SWINDON
a Born Again Swindonian's Guide

Angela Atkinson

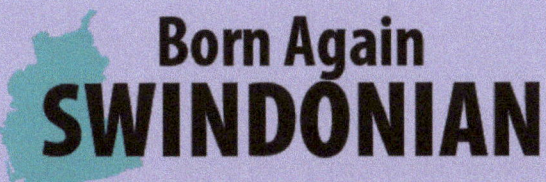
Born Again SWINDONIAN

#LookdownLookAroundLookup
www.swindonian.me

> *I think there is beauty in everything. What 'normal' people perceive as ugly, I can usually see something of beauty in it.*
> Alexander McQueen

Illustrated maps by Marilyn Trew

Photographs:, unless stated otherwise in the text:, thanks to Chris Eley

Cover Photograph by: Kate Parmaku

First published in the United Kingdom in 2020
by The Hobnob Press, 8 Lock Warehouse, Severn Road, Gloucester GL1 2GA
www.hobnobpress.co.uk
reprinted with minor corrections and additions in 2022

© Angela Atkinson, 2020, 2022
The Author hereby asserts her moral rights to be identified as the Author of the Work.

All rights reserved. No part of this publication may be reproduced, stored in a retrieval system, or transmitted in any form or by any means, electronic, mechanical, photocopying, recording or otherwise, without the prior permission of the publisher and copyright holder.

British Library Cataloguing in Publication Data
A catalogue record for this book is available from the British Library

ISBN 978-1-906978-84-6

Typeset in Gill Sans 12/14 pt
Typesetting and origination by John Chandler

GUIDE TO SWINDON

Contents

Introduction	5

Section One: Urban Discovery

Introduction — 7
1. The West Swindon Sculpture Trail — 8
2. A GWR: a History Trail — 15
3. A Central Swindon Exploration — 32
4. The Museum of Computing on Theatre Square — 42
5. The Richard Jefferies Old Town Trail — 43
6. The Blue Plaques — 47
7. A Day in Old Town — 48
8. Kids' Quiz Trails
   A New Swindon Quiz Trail — 50
   An Old Swindon Quiz Trail — 54

Section Two: Walks and green spaces

Introduction — 59
1. Hagbourne Copse and other nature reserves — 60
2. The River Ray Heritage Walk — 67
3. Secret Town Gardens — 71
4. Queen's Park — 73
5. The Coate Water Arboretum — 75
6. The GWR Park/ Faringdon Road Park — 77
7. Seven Fields Nature Reserve at Penhill — 78
8. Liden Lagoon — 79
9. Shaftesbury Lake, Eldene — 81

Section Three: Culture, Cream Teas and a Train
The Richard Jefferies Museum, 83
Coate Water and the miniature railway 86

Section Four
Messing about on the river – or rather the Wilts and Berks Canal 89

Section Five:
The Magic Roundabout 93

Appendix

A. Answers to Kids' New Swindon Quiz Trail 97
B. Answers to Kids' Old Town Quiz Trail 97

The Born Again Swindonian Guide

Introduction

In the Spring of 2013, when two-thirds of the way through a joint English Honours degree at the University of the West of England (UWE) in Bristol, I set up a blog in personal celebration of Swindon. I called it Born again Swindonian. To get the blog underway, I created a personal, non-definitive list of ten things to celebrate about Swindon. I'm unsure that I ever got that list finished, so rich a vein of material is Swindon. But that's by the by. I'm now a fully-fledged Swindon enthusiast. I'm not though blinded by the town's flaws - I simply choose to look beyond them and focus on Swindon's many positives.

After this introduction you'll find an extract from a short poem written by a good friend of mine. Now, I know she intended her words about looking for the glitter in the concrete and the sparkle in the cement as a metaphor for life, rather than a literal commentary on the urban landscape. But yet they fit well the raison d'être of this book – and that's why I've quoted them. Building on the Born Again Swindonian blog then, this book is a personal, somewhat sideways view, of things to do in Swindon that will cost you nothing or very little in terms of money. They do though need an open mind, an open heart and a willingness to look higher than eye level - and even down at the floor. But do that – and you too will see the sparkle in Swindon's cement and the glitter in its concrete. And, maybe, even the twinkle in the tarmac too – you never know.

Everything here will, I hope, give you a different Swindon experience. Thus, within these pages you won't find too much mention of Lydiard Park and house, STEAM museum or the Outlet Centre – as splendid as each of those places are. Instead you will find public art, a writer's life, a miniature railway and more.

It's often said that the best way to get to know a town is on foot. As a non-driver, on foot (and on the bus) is how I get around. It's inevitable then, that what's described in this book centres around walking and urban exploration – there's lots to be learned and seen from an urban walk I find. Ergo, everything I've included here, with the exception of the Magic Roundabout, and that's included for the craic, constitute inexpensive or free activities that I trust you'll enjoy as much as I have and do.

If we are lucky, we'll have moments in the sunlight.
when the day seems a little warmer
and the sky a little bluer.

If we are lucky, we notice the glitter in the concrete,
the sparkle in the cement
and we remember to stop and to smile ...

Carole Bent

SECTION ONE: URBAN DISCOVERY

Introduction

I **live in West** Swindon - in Grange Park to be precise – little more than the proverbial spit from the M4 junction. Developed in the 1970s and 1980s, the 11,500-home development is divided into **urban villages**. There's Toothill, Freshbrook and Grange Park with the West Swindon Centre between them and then Westlea and the town beyond. There's also Shaw Village Centre servicing Middleaze, Ramleaze and Eastleaze and, to the north of the area, Peatmoor and Sparcells.

What West Swindon lacks in old pubs, bijou bars, brasseries and indie coffee shops it makes up for with pleasantly laid out housing estates, ribboned with deep hedgerows and green spaces of every size at almost every turn, serving to remind of the green fields that existed before Swindon expanded westwards. Go up past the Shaw Ridge leisure complex - with its multiplex cinema, hotel, bowling alley, bars and restaurants - and you come to one such large green space. Once up there it's easy to forget that you're slap bang in the middle of a massive urban conurbation.

West Swindon is home to Lydiard Country Park and house, country residence of the St John family (pronounced Singun) for 500 years, and the incredible St Mary's Church next door. Though this little volume isn't the forum for going into detail about either of these buildings, suffice it to say, apropos the latter that, in 2004 and writing about St Mary's, the historian and writer Simon Jenkins observed: 'Were the south Chancel removed, lock, stock and barrel to London's Victoria & Albert museum, it would cause a sensation'.

And that sensation-causing church is here, right in our midst and is indeed a national treasure. St Mary's, like much of the development around it, sits on what was once the Lydiard estate.

Less well known about West Swindon is that it's punctuated with a series of diverse, surprising, open-air sculptures known as the West Swindon sculpture trail. The public art and the West Swindon sculpture trail were among the first things I identified as my 'Ten things to celebrate about Swindon'. Thus it's fitting that I should begin this Born again Swindonian guide with that. Because, whilst Swindon as a whole has a liberal scattering of public art across its length and breadth, West Swindon is notable for the number it has within easy walking or cycling distance of each other.

1
THE WEST SWINDON SCULPTURE TRAIL

Take the sculpture challenge: follow the map and go in search of the sculptures

THAMESDOWN BOROUGH COUNCIL commissioned the pieces that comprise the West Swindon sculpture trail in the period from the early 1980s to the early 1990s. Funding came, in part, from the housing developer's contributions to the Percent-for-Art public realm scheme. An important feature of Swindon's cultural make-up, these sculptures have neither the recognition nor attention and care that they deserve.

On the face of it then, a long walk around some admittedly neglected public art, doesn't sound like it's got much going for it. Yet this walk around West Swindon's sculptures takes in a number of children's playparks and crosses acres of astonishingly green landscape. With a little imagination, this is an activity of which you can make as much or as little as you wish. At a steady walk, and with only a passing examination of each sculpture, you could do it in a couple of hours. But why not take your time about it and make a day of it? Or a chunk of a day at least. You can try out the outdoor gym up at Shaw Ridge, have a go on every slide and swing in the play parks you pass – yes adults too! Stop for an ice-cream

GUIDE TO SWINDON

THE WEST SWINDON ART TOUR

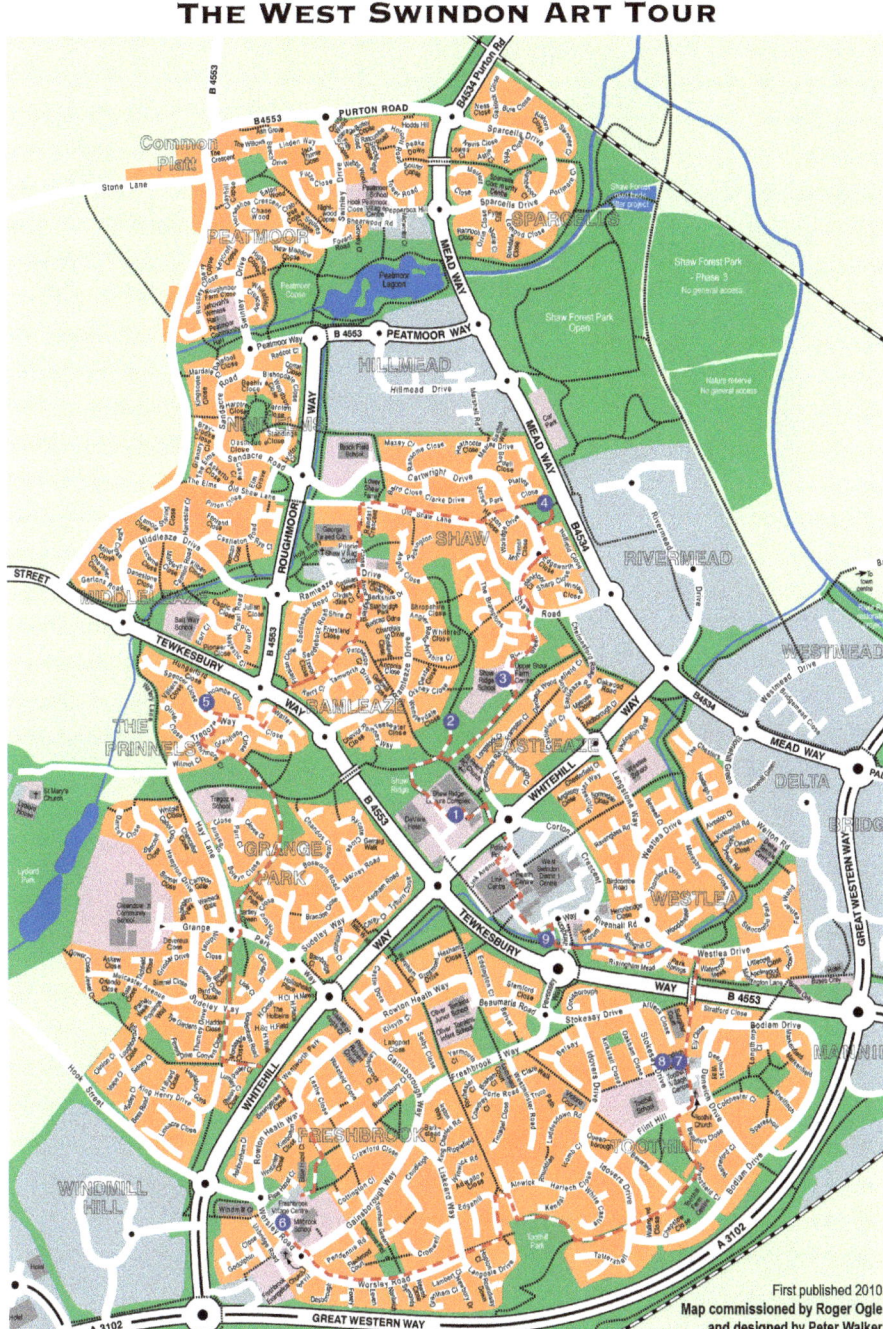

First published 2010
Map commissioned by Roger Ogle
and designed by Peter Walker

at Shaw Village centre or take a picnic.

Above all: get outside and see them and see West Swindon in a different way and in a new light.

Installed between 1982 and 1992 these sculptures sit with no explanation and often go unnoticed. They encompass a gamut of subject matter ranging from realism to abstract, including a film star and a nursery rhyme. A circular walk, approximately five miles long, will take you around all seven of them. The terrain is largely flat and family friendly – great if, like me, you're not inclined to inclines. Swindon boasts an astonishing amount of green spaces and this sculpture trail takes in some of them. There are children's play parks and an outdoor gym en route giving plenty of added interest and making it dog-friendly and picnic-suitable. It would add a new element to a bike ride too.

A good starting point for the trail is the West Swindon Centre. Here you'll find a well-known supermarket, a chain coffee shop and some fast-food chains. The Link Centre is also here. This Meccano-resembling building houses West Swindon library and a sports centre complete with ice-rink, swimming pool and tons of trampolines. Indeed, the ice-rink in the Link Centre is the home of the Swindon Wildcats ice hockey team. There is ample free parking here and the centre is well served by buses from the town centre – so it's easy to access the trail's start point.

Sculpture No 1: Diana Dors by John Clinch 1981
Appropriately located outside a multiplex cinema on Shaw Ridge leisure park (across the road from the West Swindon Centre) the first sculpture you encounter is a flamboyant bronze portrait of the late film star Diana Dors, a daughter of Swindon. Unveiled by David Puttnam this piece is a larger-than-life homage to the woman billed as Britain's answer to Marilyn Monroe. Also home to a bowling alley, a De Vere Village hotel, an Indian restaurant, a pizza restaurant and burger/ribs place this leisure complex also offers ample free parking.

GUIDE TO SWINDON

Sculpture No 2: How the Mighty Fall by Tim Sandys-Renton 1989
A few minutes' walk up a slight slope from the cinema to the top edge of the leisure park, brings you to the Shaw Ridge open space. When you reach the ridge turn right. Then go straight ahead at the crossroads of paths. Take a few paces more and you reach number two on the trail How the Mighty Fall (1989) on the left. Take a few paces more and you reach number two on the trail, **How the Mighty Fall** (1989). The creator of this cast iron and aluminium sculpture envisioned people looking at it and imagining an archaeological artefact from the 20th Century. He wanted its viewers to transport themselves into the future. A future that is now our reality. Here too you will find the outdoor gym and a children's playpark. If there's a slide then you have to go down it. It's the law.

Sculpture No 3: White Horse Pacified by Julie Livesay 1987
Carry on walking along the ridge, ignore the path on your right to Shaw Ridge School. Instead, take the next right turn on to a path which takes you across somewhat Stepford-like *Bramptons*, with a tennis court on your right. When the path emerges on to Shaw Road, cross the road and turn left. Follow the bend of the road, go straight across at the roundabout and turn right on to the next path, which leads to the third sculpture, **White Horse Pacified** (1987). Created in conjunction with the Portuguese Calouste Gulbenkian Foundation this large blue and white work is an interpretation of the chalk-cut white horses surrounding Swindon. There's a children's play area adjacent to this sculpture too.

The path sweeps around to the left behind the sculpture. Cross Shaw road again and go straight ahead on the path which crosses Hanson Close and leads on to Old Shaw Lane. Turn right on to Old Shaw Lane and follow it downhill, passing Lower Shaw Farm on the right. Ignore the left turn into Randall Crescent and take the next path on the left, which leads to Shaw Village Centre. Walk past the shops on your left, cross Ramleaze Drive and go straight ahead on the path opposite. Ignore all turnings and take

GUIDE TO SWINDON

the subway under Tewkesbury Way. When you come out of the subway you are in Walter Close. Take the second turn on the right, ignore both the right turn down to the roundabout and the left turn into Grandison Close. You are now on Tregoze Way. Instead of turning left and continuing on Tregoze Way, cross the road and you have reached the fourth sculpture, Hey Diddle Diddle.

Sculpture No 4: Hey Diddle Diddle by Vega Bermajo 1992
The walk to the fourth sculpture *Hey Diddle Diddle* (1982), takes you into Shaw Village Centre. This marks an approximate half-way point. Here you can stop for an ice-cream or even a meal in the Village Inn. This is a chain pub, so have no illusions about the fare on offer but it's a convenient and comfortable pit-stop. Set in a front garden in The Prinnels, looking towards Tregoze Way, this charming Portland stone sculpture depicts the popular nursery rhyme in a domestic setting. The part of the nursery rhyme that you see from the road is the cat. Thus, before I did this walk, I spent two decades seeing this sculpture from my bus and thinking some feline fanatic had installed it. True story.

Now, return to Tregoze Way and turn left into Whitmore Close. At the end of the close go straight ahead on to the path which traverses the open space. Take the second path on your right into Grange Park and follow this path all the way to the roundabout at Grange Park Way. Cross the road and ignore the path straight in front of you which leads to a play area. Carry on instead to the right and turn on to the next path on the left. Follow this path as it crosses Sudely Way then take the path on the left just before Lumley Close. Take the underpass beneath Whitehill Way and you are now in Freshbrook. Cross Rowton Heath Way and go straight ahead on the path immediately opposite. Follow this path until you reach a grassy area then take the main path to the right into Freshbrook Village Centre where you will see the fifth sculpture, Nexus, on your right.

Sculpture No 5: Nexus by Hideo Furtura 1986
The late Japanese sculptor, Hideo Furtura, carved the sculpture in situ, in public with hand-made tools. **Nexus** is comprised of Blue Pennant stone and railway sleepers. Thamesdown Borough Council and Southern Arts funded Furtura's residency.

As you leave Freshbrook Village Centre, turn left on to the pavement beside Worsley Road but do not cross the road. Passing Freshbrook school on your left, go straight ahead at the roundabout and stay on the pavement as Worsley Road takes a long sweep to the left to join Liskeard Way. Cross Liskeard Way and go uphill on the path immediately opposite into Toothill Park. Here you can either walk straight across on the grass to the tarmac path on the opposite side of the park or you can walk a short way on the grass to your left to join a tarmac path around the top end of the park to end at the same spot. The view from the top of the park out towards the downs is far reaching and panoramic. Follow the tarmac path downhill, cross Idovers Drive and go straight ahead, passing Toothill Farm on the right, into Stansfield Close. Turn left at the end of the close and follow the path as it goes around the edge of a small park and ends at Flint Hill. Cross Flint Hill, turn right, walk past the bus stop then turn left into Toothill Village Centre where you will find the sixth sculpture, The Watchers, in front of Toothill Church.

Sculpture No 6: The Watchers by Carleton Attwood 1982
As the name suggests, this sculpture cast in ferro-concrete and featuring a mother, father, child and dog represents guardian figures looking over the then new community.

At the opposite end of the village centre, take the path downhill between the houses which leads to the footbridge over Tewkesbury Way. Over the bridge turn left into Westlea Drive. After a short distance turn left on to the path with a stream on your right. Cross Ashington Way at the pedestrian lights and walk straight ahead on the footpath immediately opposite. Cross the footbridge on your right and you will see the seventh statue, Looking to the Future, on your left at the edge of the pond.

Sculpture No 7: Looking to the Future by John Buck 1985
Completed by John Buck, the first artist-in-residence during the development of West Swindon, this glass-fibre resin sculpture depicts three life-sized sunbathing figures relaxing at the edge of the pond. Thamesdown Borough Council, Southern Arts and Property 3 funded this sculpture.

Cross the road from here to return to the starting point – or at least to the West Swindon Centre.

NB: Both Freshbrook and Toothill village centre has shops and a pub. Toothill village centre has shops but the pub is now closed.

2
THE GWR – GOD'S WONDERFUL RAILWAY: A HISTORY TRAIL

THERE EXISTS a copious amount of written material about Brunel, Gooch and their great, Great Western Railway Works. If you seek more detail of all that, than this volume can include, then I commend you to Swindon's local studies section on the top floor of the central library. Or even the library shop in the same place. In either of those you'll find everything you need to know and more besides. This trail though, starting at STEAM MUSEUM, offers a pleasing stroll and an overview.
NB: I've based this trail on something produced by Swindon Borough Council some years ago and no longer in the public domain. I have though updated it and added to it.

Note: With this trail there is some overlap with the Central Swindon exploration and the parks and gardens entries in this book. You can always do a Pic'n'Mix of course. Everything here constitutes guidelines not hard, cold, steel, railway lines.

1841 saw the Great Western Railway Company commence construction on, what was to become, an outstanding industrial centre. It changed Swindon, Britain and, it's arguable, the world. Known by Swindonians simply as the **Works** or **Inside**, in its heyday it had 14,000 people working there. The **Works** closed its doors for the last time on 27 March 1986.

a. **STEAM Museum**

STEAM museum sits right across from Swindon's McArthurGlen Designer Outlet. The museum celebrates the men and women who toiled **Inside** - building the locomotives and those who operated and travelled on the Great Western Railway. According to Mark Child's *Swindon Book*, 'R' Shop in the locomotive works formed the bulk of the museum. 'R' Shop it seems, opened in 1846 in an area designed to house fitters, turners and machine men. It was extended in 1864.

Both English Heritage and the Royal Commission for Historic monuments (as was) participated in the conversion of 'R' Shop into a museum.

Turn left at the end of the STEAM building and walk towards the Outlet Centre.

b. The McArthur Glen Designer Outlet Centre

Arising, phoenix-like from the ashes of the old industry, is a new one – shopping. And jolly successful it is too. The Outlet Centre is, in my humble opinion, a wonderful and sympathetic regeneration of the mighty GWR Works. Wander around it and examine the beams and the pieces of engineering equipment, such as the overhead crane left in place and imagine the hot and dirty and dangerous place that the Works was – it doesn't take a big leap of the imagination.

Look towards the building with the entrance to the food court on your left and look up to see the next item of note: The Hooter.

c. The Hooter

The infamous GWR hooter makes for an excellent demonstration of my exhortation to look up. Because, out of the twenty-six years that I've lived in Swindon it was only about five years ago that I noticed it. The hooter's original home was 'R' Shop, now STEAM before they moved it to the Hydraulic House – better known as the Hooter House. You walk past this building and the hooter upon it, as you approach the Outlet Centre's food court entrance.

GWR workers' lives were strictly regulated by the sound of the hooter. Even so, many

Swindonians hold a great deal of fondness for it. There's a lovely story about local landowner Lord Bolingbroke (over at Lydiard House in West Swindon) demanding the hooter be silenced because it disturbed his sleep and his pheasants. What with him being aristocracy, the GWR doffed their virtual caps and duly complied. But, in a surprising turn of events, outraged Swindonians formed a massive petition to have the hooter reinstated. And people power, I'm happy to say, won the day.

The hooter made its last hoot at 4.30pm on March 26th 1986 when the Works closed. It kept its dying breath going until the steam ran out. You can see the twin domes of the hooter on the rooftop close to the footpath to the food court.

Now turn to face Heelis – the HQ of the National Trust. Walk alongside the building with the entrance on your left. Facing you is Churchward House.

d. Churchward House

If you approach Churchward House from its rear, you'll notice there are two large, old lanterns on it. From there you'll see a small, old stone building. This once was the stores and office of the first Work's manager – one Archibald Sturrock (1843-1849). NB: There's a small brown sign with a train on it pointing to STEAM. As you walk forward, to the right of Churchward House are rails and a piece of equipment. This is the B Shed Traverser. that was used for moving

DMUs (diesel multiple units) in and out of B Shed – at the end of STEAM. The traverser came across from the Carriage and Wagon works c1964 when the carriage side of the GWR operation closed.

Not far beyond the traverser and to the left you'll see a large set of wrought iron gates going nowhere. Constructed from old boiler tubes ready for scrapping and a relic of the GWR sports ground (opened in the 1930s and sited on Shrivenham Road) they bear the letters BRW RAA – that being an abbreviation of: British Railways Region Athletics Association. David Wilson Homes, developers of the former sport's ground, donated the gates to STEAM museum, where they now stand as a proud reminder of a glorious period in Swindon's sporting history. As you turn to leave the gates behind you, look to the wall on your left. It's pockmarked with a fascinating variety of bricked up apertures of all shapes and sizes. It's most curious.

Next ... Isambard House

e. Isambard House

Isambard House is one of the earliest buildings from the Works' first stage of development, during the period 1841-1842. Once a wheel machine shop where engine repairs took place, at present the building houses the Vet Group. Looking ahead from this point you'll see two large monochrome images. One is the iconic image of Isambard Kingdom Brunel with huge chains behind him and the other is of locomotive wheels.

f. The Historic England Archive/English Heritage National Monuments Record

The pump/engine house, the stores and the Works' first offices comprise what's now the Historic England/English Heritage National Monument's Record Centre (take your pick – it seems to morph). One can still see the original window, under the brown brick arch on the ground floor, of the first accountant's office. Above it was the Works' office and behind there, Daniel Gooch, then the locomotive superintendent, worked and slept. Joseph Armstrong, George Jackson Churchward and Charles B. Collett all made changes and additions to the General Offices as the

GWR expanded. At one point almost 2,000 people worked in this collection of buildings

Now walk left down into ... The Workers' Tunnel

g. The Workers' Tunnel

Immediately before you enter the Workers' Tunnel look up to your right. Your eyes should alight on a green painted wooden shutter with an old sign above it declaring 'Training Office/Lecture Room'. Countless stories right there. Before the erection of the Workers' Tunnel, the men had to cross the main railway line to get to work. This was a perilous undertaking and serious injuries and death were commonplace. Thus, in 1871, Joseph Armstrong built the tunnel to give employees safe passage to the Works. At 115.8 metres (380ft) long the tunnel passes beneath the main line and the buildings that were the carriage works.

Iron turnstiles once regulated the workers passing through the tunnel each day, though later they were removed to allow light vehicles to use the tunnel. Back then the road that the tunnel opens onto wasn't the busy traffic thoroughfare that you see now. There are many wonderful photographs around of this time, with the men, dressed in caps and scarves, either entering the tunnel in response to the clarion call of the hooter or spilling out onto the road at shift's end, heading straight to the Glue Pot I'll be bound. Or to The Dolphin on Rodbourne Road.

Today the tunnel serves as a link between the northern site of the GWR Works and the centre of what was New Swindon: The GWR Railway Village Conservation Area – in 2018 voted England's favourite. As you walk through, check out the pinhole light pictures of rail workers across the ages that adorn the walls of the tunnel, on the left as you walk towards the town. And the stainless-steel lettering spelling out 'Swindon Works' opposite. More than one way to interpret that methinks.

As you exit the tunnel on the New Swindon side, facing you is the *Mechanics' Institution* – the heart of the GWR Railway Village Conservation area. There's more on that elsewhere in this volume.

NB: You might at this point take a diversion and walk down past the Territorial Army building, turn the corner onto Rodbourne Road and walk on down to the Pattern Store – now the Pattern Church (under the aegis of the Diocese of Bristol) - and the turntable beyond it. Or, if you don't want to go that far, make a note to return to it later.

The Pattern Store – now the Pattern Church

Topped by huge water tanks, the Pattern Store/Church dominates the Rodbourne Road cutting. Should you be wondering what function the pattern store served, it was exactly as it sounds. The building held the drawings and papers – and three-dimensional models or patterns – associated with the railway.

This fireproof building – to protect the patterns themselves one supposes – is a 'rare survival of a purpose-built pattern store, constructed by and for the Great Western Railway Works in 1897'. It has group value with the adjacent Grade II listed engine turntable and the other listed buildings of the former GWR works to the east of Rodbourne Road. Hence its Grade II listing. On 22 July, 1896, the GWR directors agreed on a need for a new pattern store at a cost of £4,000. The old pattern stores were full to bursting and many patterns were being stored outdoors under sheeting.

During WWI the pattern store's basement was pressed into service as a canteen. In more recent years the building has done duty as a pub and as an Italian restaurant. It's now been wonderfully restored and stripped back to its original appearance by the Diocese of Bristol with the addition of a windy, twisty tubular slide that whizzes you down from the upper level to the ground floor.

The Turntable

Installed in 1902, this railway balancing turntable is also Grade II listed. The British Listed Buildings website describes it thus: 'a steel machine set in a brick lined pit. The 19.8 metre diameter steel locomotive turntable is painted in the Great Western Railway livery.' Large locomotive turntables, still in working order, are now a rare thing on the British railway system. And that's why, this one in Swindon forms part of an important group of Victorian industrial

structures in the GWR Works.

h. The Mechanics' Institution
From its inception, the Mechanics' Institution gave a social, cultural and educational heart to the railway community. The original building, foundation stone laid in 1854, housed an office, a classroom, a library and a tee-total refreshment room. There were also hot and cold baths and later a concert hall.

NB: My publication, *Secret Swindon*, carries more detail about the Mechanics' Institution and the red-letter day that was the laying of the foundation stone ceremony. At the south end of the building you'd have found the reading room and the octagonal market – demolished in 1891. During WWII the roof of the building, being the area's highest point, saw service as a fire watch point.

Though derelict for more years than enough, the Historic England Heritage Action Zone on the whole of the railway village conservation area represents Swindon's best chance to see decisive action on this socially and historically important building.

Cross the road and turn left, then right and walk down Emlyn Square to the Glue Pot pub.

i. **The Glue Pot**

The Glue Pot is the last remaining public house in the GWR Railway village – once one of three – along with the Baker's Arms and The Cricketers'. Originally built as a three-story house and shop, the building's first occupant, in the 1840s, is recorded as being a Mr Fidler, whose trade is unknown. In the 1850s one William Warner occupied it as a wool and linen drapery before the building saw conversion into a public house called **The London Stout House**.

It got its current, unusual name because of its association with the woodworkers from the nearby carriage shops.

NB: See also Section One – Item Three: A Swindon Town Centre and New Swindon Exploration

With the pub on your left, cross Reading Street. Take a right turn into the alley, past the back of a large building (now The Platform). Walk along and into the back alley (the backsie) of the Railway Cottage museum – No 34 Faringdon Road

Next: The GWR Railway Village Conservation Area

j. The GWR Railway Village Conservation Area

The GWR (Great Western Railway) village conservation area, voted England's favourite in a 2018 public poll, is one of twenty or more conservation areas in the borough. There's a number of factors that make this conservation area so important. Not least of which being that, without this, and the GWR Works, Swindon as we know it today wouldn't exist. In the GWR railway village, you'll find, among other things, what is now Central Community Centre – once the Medical Fund Society Hospital, the (sadly derelict yet ultra-important) Mechanics' Institution, the Platform (built as a barracks for single men in the first instance), Park House and the GWR Park – sometimes known as Faringdon Road Park.

Isambard Kingdom Brunel himself designed the village and named its streets after important stations on the GWR network. Though a model village in name, the accommodation was anything but. The houses looked beautiful on the outside – a deliberate ploy by Brunel to impress passengers on the passing trains. But they were overcrowded and insanitary. This was no worker's utopia. Yet, squalid living conditions aside, the GWR built houses of notable architectural dignity and planning sophistication. Superior to most contemporary artisans' dwellings they set a standard for later Swindon estates, which never offered the back-to-backs familiar in other industrial settlements.

The conservation area has been expanded to include Milton Road Baths, across the road from the Central Community Centre. Known also as the Health Hydro, the baths are hugely significant, as considered the crucible of the NHS. The Turkish baths there are the oldest, extant, Victorian Turkish baths in the world.

Next: The Railway Village Cottage Museum

k. The Railway Village Cottage Museum

Back in 1966, having bought the railway village houses from British Railways, Swindon Borough Council began to renovate some of the properties in the village. Understanding the importance of the railway industry to Swindon's development, one of the cottages, 34 Faringdon Road, underwent transformation into a living museum from the period circa 1900.

The cottage is now managed by the Mechanics' Institution Trust who run regular, volunteer-led, free tours of the railway village. They also open the Railway Workers' Cottage – an eye opener for many – to visitors. See their Facebook page for information on both. If you enter the cottage from the *backsies*, you'll come into a small courtyard with its outside privy.

The cottages in the village varied in size – many of them the classic one-up and one-down configuration. The houses were allocated on status within the Works. This cottage museum has two bedrooms and has a kitchen extension - making it bigger than was standard. It's reasonable to suppose then that this cottage housed a manager or supervisor of some kind.

Exit the cottage into the main road (Faringdon Road) and turn right – the Barracks, the next building on this trail, is on your right

l. GWR Barracks – 1849-1852

The building now referred to as **The Platform** has enjoyed a chequered history. Built in the first instance as a lodging house for single men taking up positions in the Works, it later became a family hostel (converted in 1861) and a Wesleyan chapel between 1869 and 1959. Between 1962 and 2000 this lost soul of a building served as the Great Western Railway museum – until the opening of STEAM.

As a lodging house for single men it enjoyed no success at all. There were shared common rooms and kitchen and each bedroom featured a bed, a chair and a chest of drawers. The austerity and strict regime meant that most of its occupants preferred to lodge with families in the cottages – despite the intense overcrowding.

1861 saw the conversion of the barracks into small flats to provide accommodation for the influx of Welsh families brought in to work in the new rolling mills. They eventually got their own settlement on Cambria Place.

See Section One – Item Two – a Town Centre and New Swindon Exploration.

Extensive rebuilding in 1869, saw the building consecrated as a Wesleyan Methodist Chapel – remaining as such for ninety years. The chapel celebrated the wedding of many a railway worker under its roof. The Barracks currently serves as **The Platform Youth Centre** – complete with a 30-seat train carriage used as a break out and activity room.

Walk past the Barracks on your right towards the traffic lights. Cross over, go along the front of the building on your right. This is the GWR Medical Fund Hospital.

m. GWR Medical Fund Hospital - Central Community Centre

First an armoury, 1862. Then, from 1871, the Medical Fund Hospital and Dispensary. Then a Workers' Club from 1960 until village modernisation took place in 1979.

The focal Central Community Centre in the heart of the GWR Village Conservation Area began life as a conversion from the 1862 armoury built for the newly founded XI Wiltshire Volunteer Rifle Corps. This change in use is only one example of Swindon's 'cut and paste' approach to development. This tactic saw the adaptation and sometimes relocation of a surprising number of buildings as new needs arose.

By 1871, the opening of the Sawmill and Carriage Works necessitated the long-sought Accident and Emergency Hospital. The existing military hall morphed into the Medical Fund Society Hospital, complete with operating theatre. Adjacent cottages formed nurses' housing and a dispensary. Treating diseases wasn't on the agenda at this point. The Medical fund Society physician treated such cases in patients' homes or via referral letters sent to hospitals further afield.

The building once enjoyed a formal garden frontage, enclosed by iron railings. Here nurses wheeled patients out in their beds for fresh air. Though it's a moot point how fresh said air was. What with heavy coal smoke drifting in the air, executing a gradual blackening of the village's stonework.

In the fullness of time, the facilities on offer increased. Along came accident chairs, wheelchairs and airbeds, along with trusses, elastic stockings and assorted appliances. By 1930, the need arose to sacrifice the garden to allow the hospital to grow. This loss of flower beds allowed for forty-two patient beds. And an X-Ray department and a blood-donor service. 1936 saw the addition of a nearby minor injuries A&E department added with a small operating theatre that – well operated – until the Medical Fund Hospital closed and Swindon's health care provision came from the (now demolished) Princess Margaret Hospital. The first large general hospital built under the NHS

With the front of the building behind you, cross road at traffic lights to... Next Milton road Baths.

n. Milton Road Baths – AKA The Health Hydro

This erstwhile HQ of the GWR Medical Fund Society, is now mostly known as the Health Hydro, though interchangeably as The Baths, Milton Road Baths or the Old Health Centre. The GWR installed, in 1860, Turkish Baths in the Mechanics' Institute building. These baths later (1863) transferred to an area behind the Barracks with the addition of a slipper bath.

NB: A slipper bath is a freestanding bath with one end deeper than the other. During this time, the link was forged between cleanliness and health and so bathing became important in disease prevention.

Change came in 1885 when the trustees of the GWR Medical Fund Society spent £999 on a section of the Rolleston estate, on the south side of Faringdon Road on which to build a new dispensary and swimming baths. What with the old dispensary at the back of the hospital being oversubscribed and the 1868 swimming baths being without adequate facilities and ill-located within the Works' site, the need was paramount. Opening in 1892, the Swindon architect, JJ Smith designed the building in the Queen Anne style and built it with bricks from the GWR's own brick works.

The Health Hydro is in essence four buildings. At any rate the building took place in four phases with the swimming baths being the first stage. Then came a washhouse to cope with the ever-increasing laundry load from the medical fund hospital across the road. In 1898, came washing baths, followed by Turkish and Russian Baths in 1899. The Turkish Baths in the Health Hydro now have the distinction of being the oldest extant Victorian Turkish baths in the world.

Come the 20th century other services come along. In the period between the WWI and the mid-1940s eight additional consulting rooms came into use. Along with a dental surgery, a psychological clinic, a dispensary, an ophthalmic practice, a chiropodist, a physiotherapist, a paediatric clinic, a skin clinic and a masseur.

Swindon's medical fund society, conceived by the men, for the men (and their families) and run by the men (via elected representatives) was a pioneering venture well ahead of its time.

GUIDE TO SWINDON

One that played a significant role on both local and national stages. A thing of beauty and breadth, the society was 101 years old when the NHS took it over.

The building still retains many of its original internal features, including glazed brick wall tiles, feature fireplaces and stained-glass windows.

Now walk forwards on Faringdon Road with the Health Hydro on your left. Cross the road at the traffic lights into Church Place, on your right is... Park House.

o. Park House
Now home to Business West and a range of small businesses, this substantial house of London yellow brick was built in 1876 as both a home and surgery for the use of the GWR surgeons, the Messrs Swinhoe. It was to this building that engine drivers from all over the GWR system came for their annual medical and prospective employees came here for a medical examination prior to beginning their GWR employment. At length though, the population's needs outgrew the facilities that Park House could offer, leading to the building of the Milton Road facility.

**Walk up the road, on your left is... the GWR Park
Next: The GWR Park**

p. The GWR Park/Faringdon Road Park
The GWR Park, in the centre of Swindon's GWR Railway Village conservation area began life in 1844 as a cricket ground. In that year, the GWR bought land from Lt. Col. Vilett, a local landowner. That land, to the west of the new Railway Village, between Faringdon Road and St Mark's Church became first a cricket ground and later the GWR Park – known also to some older Swindonians as The Plantation or Victoria Park.

The park played then – and still does play – a big role in the social life of the railway village residents and wider Swindon. As such it occupies a special place in Swindon's history. And in cricketing history too. Dr W G Grace played here several times during the 1890s - and found himself twice bowled out for a double-duck by a local man.

The Children's Fete
The Children's Fete is Swindon's oldest summer event – dating back to 1866. Organised by the Mechanics' Institution, it ran until 1939 (except during the Great War) only halted by the outbreak of WWII. In 2003, the Mechanics' Institution Trust revived the tradition and have run it most years since.

See also Section Two: Walks and Green Spaces.

Walk forward with the park on your left. At the end of the road turn left into Church Place. On the right is... St Mark's church

q. St Mark's Church
In a bold claim, Sir John Betjeman once described St Mark's, dedicated on the feast of St Mark on 25th April 1845, as the most loved church in England. George Gilbert Scott designed this, the first of Swindon's railway churches, in the decorated Gothic style. He later went on to design the Foreign Office, St Pancras station and hotel, Edinburgh's St Mary's Cathedral, the Albert Memorial and Swindon's Christ Church – the Lady on the Hill. The hill of Old Swindon that is.

The Reverend Joseph Mansfield was appointed first Vicar. In the north-western corner of the church stands the later addition 140ft (42.7m) tower and spire which received mixed reviews. It has though secured the church's place as a landmark within the historic area.

**NB: For more on St Mark's see *Swindon in 50 Buildings*
Next: The Cemetery**

r. The Cemetery at St Mark's
Many of the early railway workers are buried in the grounds around the church. Among them are the Works' Manager, Minard Rea (1857) and Joseph Armstrong, Locomotive, Carriage & Wagon Superintendent (1877).

With the church behind you, turn left back onto Church Place, walk forward, follow the road into Bristol

Street for the **GWR (Now UTC – University Technical College) water tower.**

s. The Water Tower
The coming of the Carriage Works brought with it a need for a satisfactory, close-by source of high-pressured water for fire-fighting purposes. Built in 1871, the water tower met that need and gave a better supply to all parts of the **Works**. Designed as several tiers of long iron columns standing one on top of the other, the tower stands almost 75 ft high. At 6' deep the tank has a working capacity of 41,000 gallons (186, 386 litres).

Having admired the recently repainted tower, turn back and go left into the backsies on the houses behind Bristol Street.

t. The Backsies
In the days before modernisation of the cottages and the installation of flushing toilets, village inhabitants had an outside privy. Each day a man would bring his horse and cart up the alleys, or backsies, between the cottages to collect the waste – or nightspoil as it was called. On your left you can still see a now-bricked-up privy access point outside No 5 Bristol Street.

In addition, the backsies also served as delivery access to the backyards where residents stored coal and wood, bought from the Works. I think they're rather beautiful. The modern wheelie bins and recycling boxes somewhat detract from the view that's true. But you can still appreciate the symmetry of the design and imagine the time when the residents kept rabbits, chickens and even pigs in their backyards. And how insanitary it all was with no shadow of a doubt.

This is the end of the GWR History Trail

3
A Central Swindon Exploration

There are those who'll tell you that there's nothing neither of interest nor beauty in Swindon's town centre. But I don't believe that's true. Follow this route, and follow the instructions in this book's introduction – the bit about opening eyes, mind and heart that is – and I trust that you'll see the beauty and the points of interest all around the town centre and the railway village area. The aforementioned glitter in the concrete.

Start at DaPaolo Italian delicatessen on the bottom of Commercial Road. I've used this independent business as a start point for the simple reason that I like the place. Paolo serves delicious Italian coffee for a little over £1. For a couple of quid you can enjoy good coffee and a cannolo. What else do you need to know?

Leaving Paolo's, cross the road to the the defunct but currently-still-standing tented market hall. Rounding the corner of the market, walk a few feet down Milton Road. Look across the road and you'll see some steps. Cross over and head for those then go straight on. That takes you down a section of Canal Walk (the old canal path) to the Cambria bridge mural. Study the steel supports on either side of the bridge and you'll see small indentations in the metal. That's where the ropes, by which horses towed the boats along the canal, have rubbed against the metal and worn it away.

The 2015 time-travelling mural is the work of Ed Russell and James Habgood of Visual Drop. It replaces an earlier mural created by Swindon-born artist Ken White in 1982. If you know Swindon at all, see how much you recognise in this new one. The mural includes many Swindon references from across the years. Dedicated to Ken, and containing a nod to his earlier mural, the mural formed part of Swindon's 175th anniversary celebrations of the GWR.

From the TARDIS on the wall column that marks the end of the mural, cross the road and enter the **GWR park in the Railway Village Conservation area**.

In this park, you'll find a WWI memorial and a small play area for tiny tots. To the left of the play area is a floor-level human

GUIDE TO SWINDON

sundial. A person stands in a position according to the month of the year. Then, assuming there is sunshine, they cast a shadow on to the correct hour stone. As you can see in the image overleaf, there are two bands of stone. This is to allow for daylight saving time.

This installation was laid in the park as a memorial to one Winnie Ockwell.* NB: The image shows the human sundial still in its original grass setting. It's since been reset into resin.

NB: See also Section One, Item 2, The GWR History Trail.

Phil King, the designer of this sundial, designed its main slab to depict, as is fitting for the GWR Park, Swindon's railway heritage. Then for each month of the year, where there's space on the stone, it shows a different aspect of that heritage. Simon Britten of the

Photo: D & M Ball

Filkins Stone Company engraved the sundial and Simon Davis of Sunclocks from Clanville, Nr Andover installed it.

*In the vicinity of the human sundial is another, unseen, memorial to Winnie Ockwell – one of Swindon's first Brownies – and that's a time capsule. In conjunction with Martha Parry and the Mechanics' Institution Trust and St Saviour's Brownies, Winnie's family put together a time capsule for burial in this location. The Brownie connection is important in more ways than one. For, not only was Winnie an early-adopter of the Brownie badge and promise, she died in 2004 – a year that marked the 90th anniversary of the Brownies being formed. The time capsule is scheduled for opening in 2104. So make a note in your diary.

If you're interested enough, you'll find a full list of the time capsule's contents in Local Studies, in the central library. Also, should you happen to be passing, copies are registered with the International Time Capsule Society in Atlanta, Georgia, USA (who knew?) and the British Museum in London.

NB: Since this photograph was taken, South Swindon Parish Council have put the human sundial into a resin base. So it now no longer disappears when the grass grows too tall!

Note the landmarks you can see from a circuit of this park: the UTC (University Technical College) and the GWR water

GUIDE TO SWINDON 35

tower, St Mark's church, Park House and even up to Radnor Street cemetery. And of course, towering over everything, the David Murray John Tower. Other things to look out for are, the WWI memorial in the park's northwest corner, the Mother Language memorial on the side of the park looking towards Faringdon Road, the locomotive wheelset and the re-cast GWR Park signage.

In recent years, in a partnership between the council and the community, with lottery funds, the Mechanics' Institute Grassroots Gardener's project have been involved with some changes to the park. As well as the play area and the sundial, they installed the four Sarsen stones, the locomotive wheelset and the gardener's shed.

Exit the park near to Park House and have a meander around the **GWR Railway Village Conservation area** - voted England's favourite conservation area in 2018 and currently an Historic England Heritage Action Zone (HAZ).

The GWR Railway Village Conservation Area
See also Item 2 in Section One – A GWR History Trail for more information on this model village, the story of which buffers

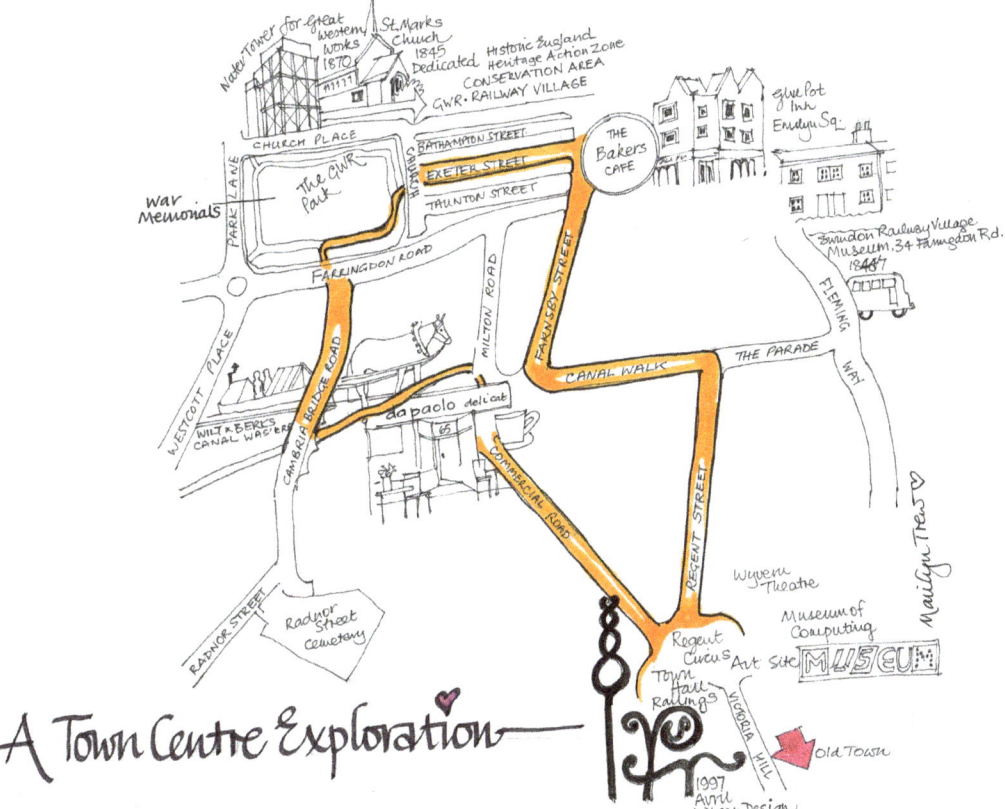

Photo: Martin Parry, Swindon Viewpoint

national and even global history. For the GWR changed Swindon, the country and the word. It certainly travelled the world.

There are good reasons to visit the railway village. In the first instance, it's pleasing enough to wander the streets, all named for stations on the GWR lines. At first glance the houses all look identical, but they're not. Those on London Road/Bristol Street differ to the rest. Wander up and down and see if you can work out why. Ignoring the modern-day intrusion of wheelie bins and recycling boxes, you can admire the symmetry of the backsies and imagine children playing there.

There are other reasons to visit the railway village too:

a   The Railway Cottage Museum
See the GWR history trail and the Facebook page of the Mechanics' Institution Trust for more infomation on the railway worker's cottage museum and their tours of the railway village.

b Refreshment Stop

Call at the last remaining pub in the village, the Glue Pot* for some good ales and ciders.

*The last one standing out of the trio of pubs in the village, the Glue Pot thrives and is a popular haunt for real ale and cider drinkers. It opened before 1850 having first been a grocer's shop. Around 1900 the pub bore the name *The London Stout House*. It morphed into being *The Glue Pot* because the coachbuilders in the Works came to the pub at lunchtime and placed their pots of the glue on the (now gone) central stove to keep the glue runny. In place of the stove is a pillar with a shelf around it on which to place your pint. Above it, on a higher ledge, is an actual glue pot – reputed to be the real deal.

See also Section One, Item 2, The GWR History Trail

c The aforementioned GWR Park

Back to Canal Walk

Having partaken of suitable refreshment, leave the Railway Village with Central Community Centre (once the Medical Fund Society Hospital) to your right. Make your way back into town via Canal Walk. As you walk down Canal Walk from Wharf Green, note what's under your feet. From Wharf Green down to the point where Canal Walk meets Regent Street and The Parade, the paving tells some history of the canal – though some of it is now obscured by the escalator going up to the food court in the Brunel Centre.

At the end of Canal Walk look for the canal milestone pointing to Semington on your left - Semington being the start of the Wilts and Berks canal constructed under a 1795 act of Parliament. This stone is a scheduled monument

Legend has it that the stone mason made a mistake with the mileage and changed the distance to Semington from 20 to 26 miles. This is a myth. It is true though that this milestone used to be on the other side of the canal, in the wall of what was then Lloyd's Bank.

At the crossroads, look left to the Golden Lion Sculpture on the polished black plinth – once a brick plinth. Examine this piece of public art and you'll see that this version of the Golden Lion was created to celebrate the 1977 Silver Jubilee of Queen Elizabeth II. Created by Carleton Atwood (sculptor), Gordon Allen (metal worker) and Edwin Horne (woodworker), the sculpture went in situ in 1978.

The recumbent lion you see now, on Bridge Street, in proximity to its junction with Canal Walk, Regent Street and The Parade, replaced the original golden lion statue that once had a precarious home above a window of a Bridge Street pub called – yep – you've guessed it - the Golden Lion. The statue's current

location is close to where that pub stood. Nor was this spot its first home - It used to bask on Canal Walk itself.

At this point, you might make a minor detour from this mapped route and nip down Regent Street towards Fleet Street. I'll admit this is not the most salubrious of Swindon's streets and areas. Yet, taking this book's ethos of looking around and looking up there's stuff worth seeing. For a start, though somewhat dilapidated, there's some interesting building facades to see. And, something I only spotted myself a couple of years back, the Burton plaques at floor level, either side of a door way on the white, curved, art-deco corner building that borders Fleet Street. This lovely, albeit sad looking building, once enjoyed life as a branch of Burton's. The plaques here mentioned commemorate the 1931 opening of the store. The names on the plaques are Raymond Burton and Barbara Burton – the son and daughter of the tailoring chain's founder, Montague Burton. From what I can gather, Burton Jnr would have been fourteen years of age when, together with his sister, he performed the opening ceremony of this branch.

Look across the road and look up and notice too, the old blue enamel sign on the building opposite. opposite. That very building has an interesting past life as a branch of the Public Benefit Boot Company and later Lennards – a shoe brand familiar to older generations.

In fact, why not venture on to Fleet Street itself? On the left-hand side, looking towards Fleming Way, amidst some admittedly uninspiring buildings, there is one rather – albeit a tad scruffy –fine upper frontage. But you wouldn't see it unless you troubled to look up. Because of course, the lower part of the frontage has, at some stage, been **modernised** – a disease that's affected and afflicted towns and cities the length and breadth of the land. At the time of writing, No. 20 is boarded up and disused. But back in the 1930s this building housed the Boys YMCA club. The lettering declaring that fact is now long gone from the building. You can see a wonderful photograph of it in its heyday on Swindon's Museum and Art Gallery flickr collection

Now, turning your feet and your eyesight back on to Regent Street, stroll up towards Regent Circus, looking up as you do so. There are several interesting building facades to see either side of this stretch of Regent Street. In particular note Marks and Spencer and the Hunter building and, towards the top on the right, the old Pearl Assurance emblem on a tall narrow building – a reminder of a long-gone insurance business. You're now at the Town Hall and Regent Circus.

The Town Hall: Take time to notice the railings around the town hall. I know that sounds like stating the flipping obvious but I can tell you that I walked past them for years and simply saw **railings**.

It was only when a friend posted a photo of them on Facebook that I *saw* them for the first time. They're a work of art in and of themselves. Installed in 1997 they're the creation of Avril Wilson, an artist-blacksmith – the first female artist to receive a bronze medal from the Worshipful Company of Blacksmiths.

If you can get in to the town hall, home of Swindon Dance, do so. For in the foyer, to the left of the doors, is a statue of Charlotte Corday – infamous for murdering Marat in his bath. There's quite a story around this statue – and here Google is your friend.

Also hidden in the town hall, the home of Swindon Dance, is a large mural by Carleton Attwood – he of the Golden Lion sculpture. The room that houses the mural is a dance studio – but you never know, if the studio isn't in use they might let you see it.

If it's a Saturday on which you're doing this meander, you could now pop into the **Museum of Computing.** See below for more about that.

But what you can do at any time is see the several murals and pieces of street art that are, at the time of writing, in that area of town. One of them, the '***Swindon: Then, when and now***' mural by Billy Beaumont is on the side of the Artsite No 9 building on Theatre Square. Indeed, the Theatre Square area has been greatly enlivened with several street art pieces. As has a dull wall on Princes Street below the Wyvern. But murals are appearing all over town so do some Googling for information. Not forgetting the My Town – my World mural by Martin Travers that runs alongside the Wyvern Theatre.

Having admired all the street art, from this point a short stroll in any direction will get you back to the town centre.

4
THE MUSEUM OF COMPUTING ON THEATRE SQUARE

SWINDON'S SMALL YET perfectly-formed museum of computing has the distinction of being the UK's first physical museum devoted to computing history. Not-for-profit and volunteer run, the museum on Theatre Square (at the time of writing) opens only on a Saturday.

There's primitive calculating devices – several steps up from the abacus mind – and the machines that led the stampede to 21st century computing. With many hands-on, interactive displays, for adults the place is a constant trigger of 'Oh gosh, I remember that' moments. And for the youngsters it's an eye-popping introduction to the days before we all had a computer in our pockets. Hard to imagine now eh?

Anyway, the museum does jolly well on Trip Advisor so they

must be doing something right. It's really a must-see for the 1980s child – with the plethora of games the museum has in its collection.

For information go to: www.museumofcomputing.org.uk

5
THE RICHARD JEFFERIES OLD TOWN TRAIL

THIS IS A circular walk that begins and more or less ends at The Square in Old Town. It's a lovely bit of urban exploration that takes you through various aspects of a writer's life and affords innumerable Old Town café/bar opportunities. Richard Jefferies, esteemed Victorian nature writer, entered the world in the farmhouse at Coate, that is now a museum to him, in 1848. He died in Sussex in 1887, from Tuberculosis, aged only 38 yrs.

Jefferies' matters for his essays depicting English rural life, his natural history books and novels. His upbringing at Coate had a huge influence on him and serves as a background to his major fiction works.

Visit http://richardjefferies.org for more information on the

museum and the man himself. See also The Richard Jefferies Society. http://www.richardjefferiessociety.co.uk, with whose kind permission this trail is reproduced. The walk begins at The Square, Old Town. Numbers refer to places on the illustrated map on page 42

1. The bakehouse and shop belonging to Richard Jefferies' grandfather, John Jefferies (1784-1868) stood to the right of the derelict and just-about-still-standing Corn Exchange (or Locarno) building. The long-since demolished shop fronted the road.

As a child, Richard visited the shop often, visiting his aunts Eliza (Sewell), Mary and Sarah.

2. Now, take the lane leading out of *The Square* along *The Weaver* and continue left into Old Mill Lane. Note the old squeeze-belly stile to your right. The path beyond the stile leads to Coate and Richard would have used it to come and go on foot. Continue along Old Mill Lane and note the buttresses in the churchyard wall. Close to this spot stood the mill, once in the charge of Richard's great uncle James. The Goddard family mansion, *Lawn,* now demolished, stood a few yards farther on.

3. On the right stands the somewhat goffick (in appearance) remains of Holy Rood Church, where Richard was baptised and where his great, grandfather Richard (1738-1825) is buried.

4. Return via The Planks to The Square and go into High Street. Note the Bell Inn – as was. Sometimes visited by the young-reporter Richard, here he'd talk with Sir Daniel Gooch and other luminaries.

Cross High Street and walk to Newport Street. By the petrol station, look hard and you'll see a plaque marking the site of the long-gone National School. During his teen years, Richard attended this school in the evenings.

    5. Take a right turn into Devizes Road. Here Richard attended two schools: Fentimans at Springhill and the Misses Cowell at Clarendon House – on the corner of Phillip's Lane. Note the ghost sign for Usher's Ales.

    Proceed along Devizes Road and turn left into Bath Road. In 1866, Number 19 was the premises of the North Wilts Herald. Under its editor, Mr Piper, the 17-year-old Richard began his journalistic career.

    6. Cross Bath Road and enter Prospect Place – where BBC Wiltshire is. Only a few houses remain dating from the 1850s. In Prospect Villas (now a car park) the Misses Cowell had a school attended by Richard in 1861.

    7. Next, enter Union Street and cut through to Victoria Road. Look for the plaque on Number 93. There, in 1875, Richard lived with his bride, Jessie Baden. Their first child, Harold entered this world at No 93. In 1877 the Jefferies' family left for London, Surbiton in fact, within the Royal Borough of Kingston upon Thames.

    8. The Swindon Advertiser, Swindon's local paper founded by William Morris (not the William Morris of Kelmscott Manor) have now vacated their offices at the top of Victoria Road. Morris was a friend to Richard and published some of his work.

    9. Cut through Union Row to Christ Church (1831) having crossed Cricklade Street. Richard's grandfather, John, is buried here. Walk into the churchyard - having reached the far end of the church, look right. There you'll find a row of Jefferies graves with round-topped headstones.

OPTIONAL – but worth the effort:
    A few yards down the road below Christ Church you'll find Chandler Close and Holy Rood School. In the grounds are three blocks of stone engraved (1989) with quotations from Jefferies by sculptor Caroline Webb.

    Return along Cricklade Street to The Square. Don't leave without visiting Wood Street – a street that Richard knew well.

Here, in rooms over 'Lay's Tearooms', at the time of writing (the building changes hands often), a bar called the **Brass Monkey**, he and Jessie stayed for a short while before moving into 22 Victoria Street (now 93 Victoria Road).

In Wood Street were shop properties owned by John Jefferies and bequeathed to Richard's aunts Fanny and Martha. Martha Hall's school was next to the King's Arms – now called *Twenty at the King's*

6
THE BLUE PLAQUES

IN RECENT YEARS a number of blue commemorative plaques have sprung up in Swindon. A walk around and across Swindon, from Old Town down to Milton Road Baths would make for an enlightening bit of urban exploration.

You can find detailed information on all the subjects of Swindon's blue plaques to date here: www.swindonheritageblueplaques.com

Thus far, in no particular order, they are:

- Edith New – suffragette
- Diana Dors – actor and film star
- The site of a Free School opened circa 1764
- The Goddard Arms in Old Town – the location of the first Masonic meeting in Swindon in 1818
- Harold Fleming – England International footballer born 1887
- The Starr Brothers. Wing Commander 'John' Starr, DFC & BAR and Sqn Leader Harold Starr killed in the Battle of Britain
- Sam Allen – lifelong Swindon Town Football club servant
- Milton Road Baths – the crucible of the NHS
- Richard Jefferies Nature Writer – the Old House at Coate
- RCAF Sergeant pilot Norman W Barbeau

7
A Day in Old Town

WHAT WE NOW call *Old Town*, should, if we're going to be formal about it, be called *Old Swindon*. Because this settlement on the hill is what comprised Swindon before the railway came and changed everything. Had Brunel and Gooch not chosen to put their GWR Swindon Works where they did, Old Town would be little changed from the sleepy market town it once was. Instead, Old Town has much to offer for both day and night-time leisure.

What follows is a planned itinerary taking in a range of elements/activities in Old Town. Of course, they're each of them discrete, stand-alone things to do - ideal if you've got a couple of hours to kill in Old Town. But if you're coming from some distance then this is one way to make the most of Old Town's undoubted attractions.

Arrive in Old Town in time for breakfast. Any number of cafes are open for coffee/breakfast. On Saturday mornings, Los Gatos on Devizes Road serves churros. There's also Jack's on Victoria Hill and Dotty's café – also on Devizes Road. This is naming but a few.

Aid digestion with a stroll around the Victorian Town Gardens.
The Town Gardens are much loved and with good reason. They're a beautiful and peaceful place to pass some time. And there's more to see than flower beds and trees – as gorgeous as they are. Wander round and seek out the aviary, the Peter Pan statue, the sundial in the rose garden and the *Victory in Europe* monument. And, should you need refreshment, there's a delightful kiosk café by the Grade II bandstand. Built in 1914, it too is Grade II listed. Built in the GWR Works as a stand for trade fairs, the kiosk straddles both Old and New Swindon.

Thamesdown Borough Council commissioned the sundial that stands in the centre of the rose garden with funding from public subscription, led by the Old Town Resident's association. Installed in 1992 it's the work of artist Marie Brett. **The sundial**

GUIDE TO SWINDON   49

commemorates one **PC Richard Webb who died too young and is engraved with the route of his beat that included Town Gardens.**

The Town Gardens are no distance at all from Swindon Museum and Art Gallery on Bath Road – see below.
*See also Section Two: Parks and Green Spaces
Take in some culture at the Museum and Art Gallery. In 1930, the one-time Toomer family home, underwent adaptation to house the various local collections – many of which date back to when Old Swindon was an insignificant agricultural hamlet on a hill. The decorative plasterwork and stained-glass details on the front windows of once family rooms, are familiar to generations of visitors to the Museum and Art Gallery. As is the gharial (Indian freshwater crocodile) on the top floor. Join the Insta crowd and post your #crocselfie tagging the museum and art gallery.

The art gallery annexe came along in the 1960s.
Or at least you could have visited the museum and art gallery. Sadly Swindon Borough Council opted not to reopen the museum when all Covid restrictions were lifted in July 2021. A large and loud

campaign has ensued and is ongoing. Plans are being mooted but there's nothing definite enough for me to mention at this point.

Follow the Richard Jefferies trail around Old Town to take in sites and things key to the life of Swindon's famous Victorian writer, the first and truest conservationist – the David Attenborough of his day.

Take a lunch break. Old Town has food for every budget and palate – from juices at The Core to bacon buttys at Dotty's café or tapas at Los Gatos – with curry, Italian and most other things in between.

Now head to *Lawn* for a stroll around the estate of the Goddard family, erstwhile Lords of the Old Town Manor. The house is long-gone, though tantalising remnants of the Goddard's Italianate sunken garden remain. Lawn is a gorgeous estate with lakes for fishing and spectacular views across the town to Highworth.

Evening: When evening comes don't rush away. Take in a show at the Arts Centre on Devizes Road or enjoy a cocktail in one of Old Town's bars, followed by dinner in any of several independent restaurants. They get busy though so it's advisable to book.

8
KIDS' QUIZ TRAILS

WITH THANKS TO Beat the Street Swindon for sharing with me their quiz trails for children, on which I've based the two trails that follow.

NB: Parents: the answers to these quiz trails are in the Appendix at the back of the book.

A New Swindon Quiz Trail

1. Start at Central library on Regent Circus. There's a monument by the library.

GUIDE TO SWINDON

Q. What is it and what dates are listed on it?

2. From there walk to the top of Regent Circus and look for The Savoy pub.
Q. Who was born here?

3. Now walk down Regent Street, studying the buildings as you go.
Q. What are Hunter's initials?

4. Turn left at Beaverbrook's jewellers onto Havelock Square. There's a statue there.
Q. Who is the statue of? And on what date did the shopping centre open?

5. Now walk towards Wharf Green. Go through the underpass/car park.
Q. Where does the Southern Flyer cycle path start and end?

6. Go up the steps. Cross the road safely and turn right. Walk down the road to Milton Road baths.
Q. What was this building the blue print for? Where does it tell you that?

At this point you could stop, return to town and do the rest of this quiz trail another time. Or, if you want to carry on ...

7. Use the crossings to get to the GWR Railway Village Conservation area. Walk through the GWR park (also called Faringdon Road park) to the WWI memorial in the park's north west corner. Leave the park at the exit there. On your left is a military building – the Territorial Army.
Q. How many rifles are associated with B Company?

8. Cross the road, take a right turn and walk down Rodbourne Rd, towards the Pattern Church, on the same side as the Outlet

GUIDE TO SWINDON

Centre. Go under the railway bridge and continue walking along the perimeter/edge of the Outlet Centre.
Q. How many aitches/Hs can you count in the arches you walk past?

9. Keep walking along Rodbourne Rd and around the corner to the food court entrance to the Outlet Centre. There you'll see a wheel set cast in the GWR works.
Q. What was the diameter of the largest drive wheels made in the GWR works? And what type of locomotives were they for?

10. Just beyond the wheel set, stainless steel words are set into the paving.
Q. How many vowels can you count in those words?

11. Take a left turn and go past the National Trust building, following the line of trees and walk towards STEAM museum. Walk past the lanterns on the back of Churchward House. Alongside Churchward House are some tracks and a piece of equipment called a traverser.
Q. What date was the traverser made?

12. Further on from the Traverser and to the left there's a large set of gates going nowhere.
Q. What are the letters on the gate? And what do they stand for?

13. Now follow the red brick path, past Isambard House, towards the GWR Workers' tunnel. Above the sign directing you to the tunnel, you'll see a green painted shutter/door.
Q. What happened in there?

14. Go through the workers' tunnel. Turn left at the exit, go to Emlyn Square. Cross at the crossing to the Glue Pot pub. Opposite you is a large stone building that was once barracks for single men working in the Works before it became a chapel. But …

Q. What is at number 34 Faringdon Road?

15. Use the crossing to get back towards town again. Turn left towards the Holiday Inn until you get to the bottom section of Regent Street looking towards the town. On a building there, there's a mythical creature looking down at you.
Q. Where is it and what is it?

16 At the crossroads between Regent Street, The Parade and Canal Walk there is a sculpture of a golden lion.
Q. Where was the other Golden Lion?

You're now back in the town centre and have reached the end of the trail. Well done!

B The Old Town Kids' Quiz Trail

This trail starts at the Swindon Arts Centre on Devizes Road (Old Town Library) – NB: it's not open on Sunday.

1. There's a piece of public art/sculpture outside the Art's Centre.
Q. What is it called? And who made it?

2. Cross at the lights and walk past the Salvation Army building.
Q. Fill in the blank in the ghost sign: Usher's Ale & _____ on Phillips Lane

3. Keep walking down Devizes Rd towards Newport Street.
Q. Which building has old-fashioned lanterns on it?

4. Continue down Croft Road and turn right into Springfield Road.
Q. Which bright-coloured flowers decorate the houses?

5. As you progress down the road, you'll see a building with an emblem of a stag on it.
Q. Who or what is the badge for?

GUIDE TO SWINDON

6. Continue along the road and through the gates to the town gardens. Close to the gates is an aviary.
Q. How many birdboxes does the aviary have?

7. Head beyond the bandstand and you'll see a statue of a child – it is in fact the fictional character, Peter Pan.
Q. What lies between his feet?

8. Go through the first set of gates.
Q. What is the middle house/building for?

Now continue via the second set of gates and leave the park via the play area exit. Turn left and **be careful** going up the hill, look out for cars coming down.

9. Turn right and head back towards Old Town centre.
Q. Which house is next to Victoria House?

10. Cross at the first lights and continue towards Old Town. There's a terracotta creature sitting on the corner of the roof of a large, stone-built building.
Q. What is the building?

11. From the building in question 10, continue down Bath Road to the building that corners with Victoria Road.
Q. Who would have answered the bell?

12. Go past the building in question 11, down the slope, cross at the lights and turn left.
Q. When did No. 100 get the 'Borough of Thamesdown Conservation Award'?

13. Continue down the hill looking to your left.
Q. At which number building do you see some black and white floor tiles in the entrance?

14. Now, carry on down the hill a little. Turn right at **The Victoria**, onto **Union Row.** Head for Christ Church which you can see up ahead of you. So long as there's no weddings or funerals going on, enter the church for the answers to the next two questions:
Q. How many people are the main, front doors dedicated to?

Study the stained-glass windows. One of them has a dog's head with red stripes on it.
Q. What colour is his companion in the window?

15. Now leave the church via the side door on the right. Notice the small stained-glass window commemorating the GWR. Walk straight ahead to the graveyard and look for a grave with a Celtic cross on it.
Q. Who is buried there?

16. Now double back on yourself and head for the gates off to the left, past the beloved wife of Thomas Turner. Turn left towards the Goddard Arms.
Q. When was the first Masonic meeting held there?

17. Cross at the lights and head into Wood Street. Look for the pub, 20 at the King's.
Q. What animal do you see with the unicorn?

Continue left, back to the Arts Centre. Congratulations! You've completed the Old Town quiz trail.

SECTION TWO: WALKS AND GREEN SPACES

Introduction

ONE THING YOU'LL often hear said of Swindon, apropos its positive attributes, is its position in the midst of much wonderful countryside. And that's true. I don't deny it. There's the Marlborough Downs, The Ridgeway, the various white horses on various hills, Avebury, Stonehenge and Salisbury Plain to name but a few. But yet, but yet, but yet – you do not have to leave Swindon to enjoy more nature and greenery and wildlife than you can shake a Nordic walking pole at. Indeed, on that note, and in conversation not so long ago, with a chap from Wiltshire Wildlife Fund, he observed two things:

1. How underestimated Swindon is in general
2. How underestimated it is in terms of green spaces and wildlife

And his argument is compelling. It is. So, what follows are a mere few of the wonderful green spaces, open spaces, walks and nature reserves that cut through the heart of Swindon. And if you only ever cross Swindon by car and never venture out on foot or on bicycle you'll miss the joys they contain within..

1
Hagbourne Copse and other West Swindon Nature Reserves

WERE IT NOT for social media I might never have heard of Hagbourne Copse. A picture of a friend, surrounded by bluebells, that appeared on my Facebook timeline prompted me to ask: 'Where's that then'? Back came the reply, Hagbourne Copse and a description of where to find it. 'Blimey – that's just up the road from me. I had no idea.' But then this is not a place you'd pass on the way to anywhere. You need to know it's there. The best time to visit it is in late April / early May when the floor is covered in a thick-pile, bluebell carpet. This little piece of ancient woodland, tucked away in the corner of an industrial estate is a total delight. All the more so for being so unexpected.

The Wiltshire Wildlife website (www.wiltshirewildlife.org/hagbourne-copse-swindon) tells us that the copse was planted some time before 1766 and belonged to the Lydiard Park estate. Wiltshire Wildlife bought the copse in 1999. Volunteers continue to work coppicing trees to produce new shoots and carry on the age-old tradition of harvesting wood.

How to find it

By car: Hagbourne Copse is in the Blagrove Industrial Estate. From M4 junction 16 take the A3102 towards Swindon. At the roundabout turn right into Ramsden Road. At the next roundabout turn right into Frankland Road. The entrance is on the right before the T-junction. There is some parking along Frankland Road.

Cycling: On the Sustrans website you can find Swindon cycle map routes. There's one that runs adjacent to Hagbourne Copse. www.sustrans.org.uk

Photo: Roger Ogle

Also worth visiting while you're in the West Swindon area:

Lydiard Park and House (1 mile)
www.lydiardpark.org.uk

As I said in the introduction, this isn't the place to go into too much detail about Lydiard House and park. There are plenty of other sources for that, not least of which is their own website – see URL below. But to give you a brief overview: At the heart of the lovely Lydiard Park is Lydiard House. This striking Grade 1 Listed Palladian house provided a home for 500 years to the St John (pronounced Sinjun) family. The beautifully restored state apartments on the ground floor are open to visitors. There aren't a great number of rooms to see but there's a collection of impressive paintings and objects within them. There are audio guides in each room. Or bag a member of staff for a guided tour if you can. Some of them are very knowledgeable.

Among the highlights of the house is a dressing room that celebrates Diana Spencer – ancestor of the Diana Spencer that modern Britons know as the Princess of Wales. The resemblance between the two is striking. If ever you thought that the downcast

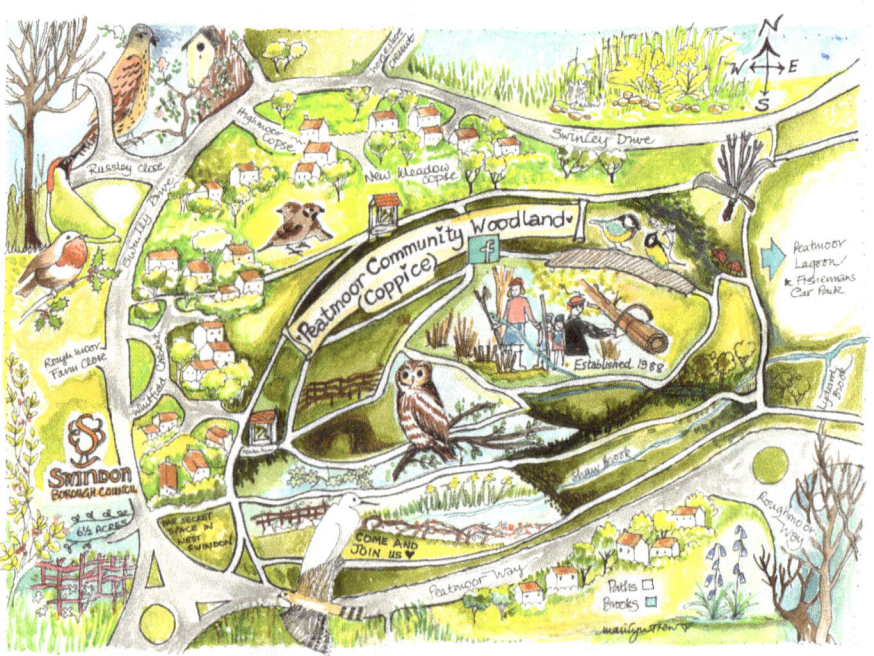

eyes thing that the Princess of Wales was wont to do, was an affectation, you're mistaken. You can see the same expression in this portrait. In this room you can also see a rare and very beautiful 17th century painted window and a mechanical desk made by Giovanni Socchi in the early 19th century.
For more information visit: www.lydiardpark.org.uk

Peatmoor Community Woodland

This community woodland formed in 1988 when Swindon Borough Council (then Thamesdown Borough Council) invited residents to participate in the traditional management of a six-acre copse within the town's western expansion, close to the newly created Peatmoor Lagoon. The wood is a remnant of the ancient Bradon forest – a royal hunting forest that covered most of north Wiltshire for hundreds of years. During the 18th Century, much of the land was cleared for agriculture but the copse survived to provide

Photo: Roger Ogle

wood for fencing and fuel. From WWI the area fell into disuse as less labour intensive and more accessible materials were used for agriculture and construction.

It's known that the Romans used coppicing to manage trees. And, what the ancients started, volunteers continue in much the same way with an emphasis on caring for the ecology of the site and maintaining an educational amenity. With the health of the planet riding high on the public agenda, Peatmoor Community Woodland is a tiny, but locally important, element in mitigating climate change. As a wet woodland, never cultivated for crops, the soil consists of several metres of accumulated organic material in what is known as a carbon sink – trapping CO_2 in its structure.

You can visit the woodland at any time. Note though that because the site is kept in a very basic state, paths are uneven and muddy in the wetter months. The nearest facilities are 800 metres away at Peatmoor village centre.

For more information visit: www.bit.ly/peatmoorcopse

Shaw Forest Park

At the time of writing, Shaw Forest Park is a 40-hectare community woodland situated about 3km north-west of Swindon's centre. There are several footpaths from the park to Sparcells, Hillmead, Ramleaze and Eastleaze. A major cycle route links the park to Rivermead (managed by the Wiltshire Wildlife Trust), Mannington Rec. and the town centre to the south. Then Moulden Hill, Rodbourne Cheney and Priory Vale to the north.

On the Buses: The closest bus stop is by the entrance ramp to the park opposite the Vauxhall Scurry's Garage. Bus numbers 22 and 18 stop there.

Moulden Hill Country Park

This country park lies to the north-west of Swindon town centre within the parish of Haydon Wick – though it is owned and managed by Swindon Borough Council. Close to Thamesdown Drive, the park has footpaths and a hidden lake.

Barbury Castle Country Park (5 miles)

Barbury Castle is not what the word 'castle' invokes. There are no battlements and steep, spiral staircases here. Though there is a moat of sorts – visit and you'll see what I mean. And there's sheep – that's the baaa facts of the matter. Sheep and moats aside, what you have here is a 60-hectare, iron-age hill fort notable for its chalk grassland and associated wildlife overlooking Swindon. Indeed, the views are spectacular. The thin soil has good drainage where specialist plants grow. And did I mention sheep? This is an isolated spot that makes great walking, wildlife watching, kite flying, mountain biking and horse riding.

Getting There: Barbury Castle lies about three miles south-west of Chiseldon. From Junction 15 on the M4 follow the A346 towards Marlborough looking for signs for Chiseldon. Then follow signs for Barbary Castle. From Swindon take the A4361 (Croft Road) towards Wroughton. At the junction by the Morrison's store, take the B4005 towards Chiseldon. Then follow signs towards Barbury Castle. There's a car park with a toilet block and an amenity field next to it for dog exercising

Cherhill White Horse and Avebury (8 miles)

There's lots of information about this and the seven other Wiltshire white horses on the Visit Wiltshire website here: www.visitwiltshire.co.uk/things-to-do/cherhill-white-horse-p1692613. So I'll simply say that: The Cherhill (pronounced Cheryl) White Horse, sometimes called the Oldbury White Horse, lies on the edge of Cherhill Down. It's near both Oldbury Castle and the Landsdown Monument - three and a half miles from Calne.

Avebury

You'll find this stone circle, museum and manor house in the heart of the Avebury World Heritage site. The Avebury complex is numbered as one of the main Neolithic sites that you can still visit today. Built and altered over many centuries it's one of the largest and most complex of the surviving Neolithic Henges in Britain. Archaeologist, Alexander Keiller excavated in Avebury in the 1930s and the museum there bears his name. For more information visit: www.nationaltrust.org.uk/avebury

Fyfield Down National Nature Reserve (8 miles):

Fyfield Down National Nature Reserve, Manton House Estate, Marlborough, Wiltshire, SN8 1PN. Created in 1955, this is one the country's oldest National Nature Reserves and forms part of the Avebury World Heritage Site. For more information visit: www.nationaltrail.co.uk/ridgeway/attractions/fyfield-down-national-nature-reserve

Other nature reserves close by:

Rushey Platt
Swindon SN5 8ZQ
OS map 169 Grid ref: SU136835

The Rushey Platt reserve is a remnant of the lush wetland marsh that once covered much of south Swindon. Until that is land drainage rendered this type of habitat unusual in Wiltshire. Sandwiched between the River Ray, Wilts and Berks Canal and the former Old Town railway line, it's a vital area for wildlife where you can enjoy a quiet walk.
Visit the Wiltshire Wildlife website for more information: www.wiltshirewildlife.org/rushey-platt-swindon

Swindon Lagoons
Swindon SN5 7ET
OS map 169 Grid ref: SU124859

The wonderful Swindon Lagoons represent nature's incredible ability to recover from man's excesses and effluent. Until 1985, Thames Water used the lagoons to store waste by-products from their treatment works. When they cleared them out, they were planted with reeds. Under the management of Wiltshire Wildlife, wildlife fills the lagoons once more. The reserve lies behind a security fence but you can visit it on guided tours and open days.

GUIDE TO SWINDON

Why not book on one and enjoy a walk around the fifteen lagoons, reed beds, grassland, marshland and a stretch of the River Ray? NB: The River Ray Heritage walk that you come to next in this book takes you past these lagoons.

For more information visit:
www.wiltshirewildlife.org/swindon-lagoons-swindon

2
THE RIVER RAY HERITAGE WALK

SWINDON ARTIST, Marilyn Trew made the maps, accompanying this walk description, from the original leaflet made to promote this walk, back in the 1980s. You can see the original in the Local Studies section of Swindon's Central Library. I've recreated it with their kind permission (see www.swindonian.me for River Ray Parkway posts). This walk is a super example of the views, the greenery, the nature and the wildlife hidden in Swindon's heart.

The River Ray Parkway is a green walking and cycling route. Introduced to the town in 1991 as part of the Great Western Community Forest scheme, it runs for eight miles from Coate Water to Moulden Hill. Or in reverse. The walk expanded from an original effort to create the Swindon Old Town Rail Path, developed with the help of Sustrans – then a small Bristol group formed to create better walking and cycling routes.

Today, the route is mostly maintained as National Cycle Network Route 45 – started by Sustrans with a National Lottery grant in 1995. The purpose built NCN (National Cycling Network) signs are quite obvious in the landscape – the old green heritage signs rather less so. Should you live or ever have wandered in the south-west/south-east parts of Swindon you may have encountered, here and there, these dark green metal signposts in various states of disrepair. Some of them have lost some of the arms/pointers and some of them are little more than stumps. Note that, where the pointers on the signs do still exist, it's inadvisable to put too much faith in them as many have been turned around by mischief makers.

The River Ray Heritage Walk: Part One

I did this walk with a friend and we did it in reverse – starting at Moulden Hill. As indicated above, the dark green Parkway signs tend to blend into the landscape – a bit of a design flaw there – so it took us a while to spot one. Having decided to start at Moulden Hill, from leaving the roads we walked along a leafy corridor. We spotted our first Parkway sign as we were almost at Shaw Forest Park – shown as Shaw Tip on the River Ray Parkway map.

From here the route follows the edge of the Shaw Forest Park. It goes past the Swindon Lagoons described earlier. There are signs describing the habitat of the lagoons that are readable through the fence. Doing this walk was the first I knew of these lagoons – I rest my case about what you see if you get out of your car. There's even an old kissing gate down here.

Continuing south-east, the walk catches up with a tributary of the River Ray. If you're short enough (I am!) you can follow it underneath the Great Western Way dual carriageway. Then it goes around the expansive Mannington Rec sports ground and park and the Bridgemead Retail Park. From the map, you'll notice that the River Ray Parkway follows two routes from Royal Wootton Bassett

GUIDE TO SWINDON

Road to Rivermead.

The western route follows the western tributary of the River Ray, via Westlea Park and alongside Westlea Primary school. It follows the current NCN route 45, and the Western Flyer, a newer route created to provide a cycling-commuter route into the town centre. When my companion and myself did the walk, we did the eastern route and rounded the whole thing off with coffee and cake in John Lewis. So, when we came to do the second half we started there and proceeded forth to the end/start point at Coate Water. Suitably hungry and thirsty we headed to the Sun Inn at Coate for food and beer.

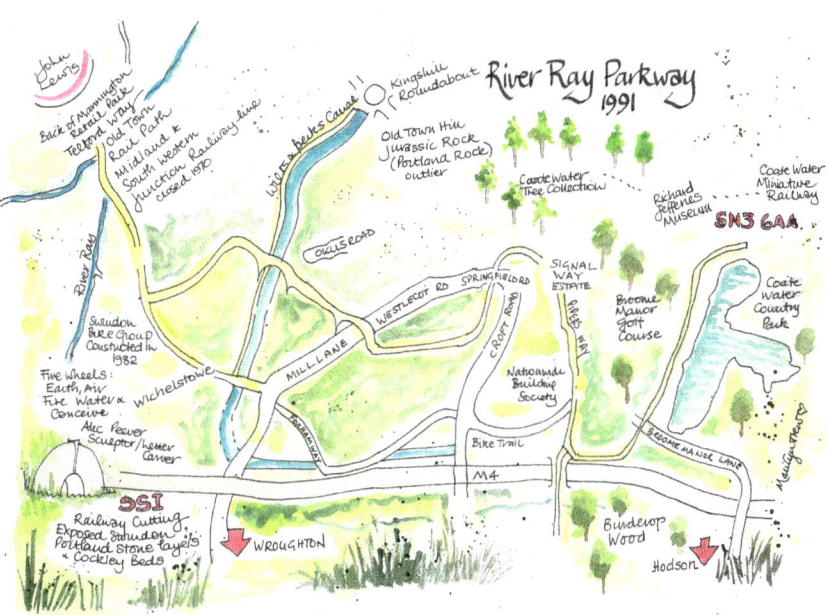

The River Ray Heritage Walk Part Two

Leave the back of Mannington Retail Park and look for the old green signs pointing the way you need to go. You'll find the first one on the edge of a field used by dog walkers. It points towards the Old Town Rail Path, following Sustrans Route 45.

The Parkway continues along the Old Town Rail Path, the former route of the Midland and South Western Junction Railway

(Swindon's other railway), closed in 1970. Along this path there are five wheel sculptures all looking rather the worse for wear. The first wheel, "conceive", is graffitied but still readable. It bears the message: "Stepping out of character, you interrogate a chaos of bearings. Where is the unknown journeyman, with his bag of fives, his measuring rod and chisel"

The route passes all the wheels and affords some simply wonderful views out over the south edge of Swindon.

Near the end of the rail path, the cutting gets deeper and passes under Westlecot Road. At this end, the path is a Natural England, designated site of special scientific interest, as it shows all the layers of rock upon which Swindon sits.

Shortly after that, the walk passes under another bridge, with Devizes Road and the Plough Inn on top of it, out of the cutting and into the light again.

The route now follows the road through the Signal Way industrial estate, sneaks out at the end of Berenger Close (quite tricky to find) and over the top of Evelyn Street, still following the old railway line. From the sign, head south along Piper's Way, crossing over to take the off-road path around the allotments on the east side. Shortly after the allotments a further sign points off-road onto a track that leads all around the edge of the Broome Manor Golf Complex.

On this track there's a stone marker, planted in memory of Cassandra Clunies-Ross, carved by Sarah Chanin in 1992. The work is carved in Sarsen stone and was commissioned by Thamesdown Borough Council's, Great Western Community Forest Team. The stone marks an area of what was then new woodland. The inscription on the stone reads: 'Casso's Wood – planted January 1992 by friends, in fond memory of Cassandra Clunes Ross, ecologist-forester. 1965-1991. That her work to conserve woodland here and abroad is not forgotten.'

The last stretch of the trail narrows and squeezes past nettles and other flora and fauna. Then suddenly it finds Broome Manor Lane and the Coate Water Park.

The final Parkway sign stands to the west of the lake, near the miniature golf course and points to:

- Lydiard Country Park
- River Ray Parkway
- Cycle Route
- Broome Manor Lane
- Visitor Centre
- Chiseldon

3
Secret Town Gardens

Aside from the obvious attractions of Town Gardens described in the *A Day in Old Town* itinerary, there are a few hidden, less well-known things to look for in the town gardens to add another element of interest to your visit. The illustrated map will guide you to them, as will the instructions below:

Use the sundial described earlier, in the centre of the rose garden, as a start point for this little treasure hunt of sorts. Move forward from there to the Peter Pan statue and, just ahead and to the left, the Victory in Europe monument. On a right diagonal, ahead of the VE monument, if you look carefully you'll see a stone gate pier, on Quarry Road corner, attached to railings. Walk right up to it and you'll see a small head on the pillar with a sad face. But it wasn't always so. It seems that the mouth on the face once turned up in a smile until, many years back now, bored/mischievous boys got to work with their penknives and made the mouth turn down.

Now, with the gate pier behind you, walk along the path studying the benches. Look for the Tinkerbell bench – the brass commemorative plaque on the bench references the fairy from Peter Pan.

Behind that bench and up to the right is a mound. It doesn't like look anything other than a mound. But that mound used to be a magazine store – for explosives for the quarry. Because a quarry is

what Town Gardens once was. When the site functioned as a quarry no more, the leisure gardens we enjoy now were born from it.

Now double back to the VE Monument and cross the park to the steps taking you to the bowls club and the handkerchief tree. Properly known as *Davidia involucrata*, this tree gets its nickname from the handkerchief shape of its blossom. I've also heard it described as little ghosts – I rather like that. From there, go through the gates and to the left. Walk along a little and you'll see a remnant of the quarry where you can see the strata of the Swindon stone.

NB: Should you be able to get into the area immediately in front of the concert bowl (it's locked when the bowl is not in use) look at the steps to the left of it – you should be able to see, embedded into the wall alongside the steps, some ammonite fossils.

4
Queen's Park

WITH THANKS TO France Bevan's blog *Swindon in the Past Lane* for most of this information about Queen's Park. Wander around Queen's Park and try, if you can, to conjure up the image of this site as it used to be. For this 12-acre, parkland sanctuary from the hustle and bustle of Swindon town centre arose from a brownfield site. The ponds, the flower beds and the trees all belie the park's industrial past as the site of Thomas Turner's (1839-1911) brick works – and I'll come back to him in a moment.

Nowadays, the once derelict claypit is a Grade II listed park, developed between 1947 and 1962. The then Princess Elizabeth (now The Queen) opened the first phase in 1950 – the year of Swindon Borough's Golden Jubilee - a Garden of Remembrance to the fallen of WWII. Later, in 1953, Sir Noel Arkell, in his capacity of Sheriff of Wiltshire, opened the second phase. Queen's Park continues as a place of remembrance via the Mesothelioma Memorial Garden opened by the then Mayor, Stan Pajak in 2003. Mesothelioma is otherwise known as the 'Swindon Disease', caused as it was by exposure to the asbestos in the GWR Works. The long-time resident gorilla sculpture, by Tom Gleeson, took up his post in Queen's Park in 1994, following a tenure in Theatre Square in the mid 1980s.

A mere hop, skip and jump from the town centre, Queen's Park has several entrances. There are entrances off Groundwell Road and at the bottom of Durham Street, with its main entrances being off York Road and Drove Road. And Drove Rd brings us back to Thomas Turner. A tangible reminder of Thomas Turner and his Swindon Tile and Pottery Works are the two houses beside Queen's Park's eastern entrance. Known colloquially as the Catalogue Houses they feature a range of brickwork and decorative motifs – designed to show off Turner's repertoire of bricks and embellishments. I assume then, that, were you in possession of the wherewithall to have a house built for you, you'd toddle along to Drove Road, decided which brickwork took your fancy and you'd place your order with the eponymous brick work owner. See Swindon in 50 Buildings for more on these two villas.

The Drove Road entrance to Queen's Park is not so far from Old Town. So, if you've been in Old Town following, say, the Richard Jefferies Old Town trail, why not extend your walk down to this urban oasis? And/or whip your smart phone out of your pocket and call up Google maps and go looking for houses bearing Thomas Turner features. You'll find typical Turner decorative features in Belle Vue Terrace, Hunt Street and Turner Street (named after our man) off Westcott Place. These houses were built with his own bricks as were other streets linking New Swindon and Old Town. On those houses and on others he built in Lansdown Road, Kingshill and Westcott Place you'll find a repeated pottery plaque or keystone in the form of a bearded man surrounded by shell motifs and running vines. It's said that this face is the likeness of Daniel Lynch, a worker at Turner's Stratton St Margaret brick, pottery and tile yard.

5
The Coate Water Arboretum – Coate's Tree Collection

NB: For information on Coate Water country park in general see Section Three

On entering Coate Water from the main car park, you take a left towards the miniature railway and the play park or walk right, in front of the toilet block to the mini-golf and the pitch and put. But what fewer people do is take a right turn, behind the toilet block and walk into and around the Coate Water Arboretum. Planting of this collection of trees from around the world began in the winter of 1982/1983. Maurice Fanning, a former Mayor of Swindon performed an official opening on the 15 April 1998 of this diverse collection of specimens. Though some of the trees in the collection have now lost their labels, the trees are all still there spread over Spring Field, Oak Field and Quarry Field.

There are actually a number of access points to the tree collection, the main one, as described above, is via the main car park at Coate Water. Should you not be so steady on your feet you can still see the tree collection as you can hire a suitable mobility scooter from the ranger station. Their contact details are:

Tel: 01793 490150; Email: swindonrangers@swindon.gov.uk

Coate Water Park
Marlborough Rd
Swindon SN3 6AA

For more on Coate Water see Section Three: Culture, Cream Teas and a Train

NB: See also Section Three

6
THE GWR PARK/FARINGDON ROAD PARK

THE GWR PARK, in the centre of Swindon's GWR Railway Village conservation area began life in 1844 as a cricket ground. In that year, the GWR bought land from Lt.Col.Vilett, a local landowner. That land, to the west of the new Railway Village, between Faringdon Road and St Mark's Church, became first a cricket ground and later the GWR Park – known also to some older Swindonians as The Plantation or Victoria Park. Aside from cricket, the park played – and still does play – a big role in the social life of the railway village residents and wider Swindon. As such it occupies a special place in Swindon's history.

Sadly, the ornamental, formal gardens, along with the cricket pavilion, the bandstand and glasshouses are long gone. The park does though have a small play area for tiny tots and, installed in November 2018, in the park's northwest corner, a WWI memorial. It affords a peaceful spot for some quiet contemplation. What makes this park stand out for me, aside from its location in the GWR Railway Village conservation area, is what you can see from it. As you walk around the park you can see the water tower and UTC, the school, St Mark's Church, Park House and up to Radnor Street cemetery. And of course, towering over everything, the David Murray John Tower.

7
SEVEN FIELDS AT PENHILL

IF THIS LITTLE volume is meeting its aims, you should by now see that Swindon is a town of surprises and hidden gems. The Seven Fields nature reserve at Penhill, north Swindon is yet another example of such. In similar fashion to being on West Swindon's Shaw Ridge, a look southwest from Penhill's Winterslow Road offers the same abiliity to forget the urban conurbation all around you.

Comprising over 100 acres, the Seven Fields Nature Reserve occupies a valley to the west of Penhill between Haydon Wick and Abbey Meads to the north. Rich in wildlife, Seven Fields boasts some of the best wildflower meadows in Wiltshire along with ancient hedgerows, a stream, a Wild Service Tree (*Sorbus torminalis*) and an ancient woodland called Penhill Copse. It received a Local Nature Reserve Designation in 1995. Recorded in the meadows are a rich variety of flowers and grasses. This range of plant species creates crucial breeding and feed stations for butterflies, moths, grasshoppers and all manner of creepy crawlies. Under the ownership of Swindon Borough Council and the care of Haydon Wick Parish Council the reserve gets its name for obvious enough reasons.

For a full description of each field visit:
https://haydonwick.gov.uk/seven-fields/

8
LIDEN LAGOON

FURTHER PROOF, IF further proof were needed by now, of what is hidden away in plain sight is Liden lagoon. I mentioned earlier that I live in West Swindon – a particularly verdant area of the town. And I'd rather harboured the impression that some of Swindon's older suburbs – like Liden and Eldene had nothing much to offer in terms of green spaces. How wrong was I? Both Liden lagoon and Eldene's Shaftesbury lake truly fit the whole hidden gems thing. You can whizz along the A419, in blissful ignorance that below you, on your left as you head towards Liden, is the lovely Liden lagoon, tucked away in a housing estate.

At the official entrance to the lake there's a monumental stone entitled Country Seats Telling Tales – that's engraved with a map of the lagoon. There are Sarsen stones scattered around the edges of the lake and a shaded walking path dotted with fishing platforms. When I visited there was a veritable gang of geese, that I took great care to circumnavigate, and more than one swan stalking about like it owned the place – which I suppose it does.

Around the perimeter of the lake are numerous benches with a short water related poem/aphorism carved into them. One such being: Heron so still at the water's edge.

Built as a flood storage facility during the development of the South Dorcan extension, between the late 1960s and early 1980s, the lagoon is a delightful spot that offers both habitat for an assortment of water birds and a leisure resource. It's fed by the Liden brook which flows down from Liddington. You can see this brook should you go through the woods near Liddington Manor. The lagoon is, I believe, a flood storage facility for Coate Water run-off, built during the development of the South Dorcan Extension of the late 1960s to early 1980s. It provides a habitat for various water birds and a leisure resource. This a view to the north-east.

9
Shaftesbury Lake – Eldene

WHERE LIDEN LAGOON exists by design, the splendid Shaftesbury Lake is something of a happy accident. Early photographs (1960s) of the area, before the building of the estate, show no naturally occurring lake. By 1966, Park South and Park North were built and construction of Eldene begun. Because Eldene is atop a hill a receptacle was needed for rainwater runoff. The clay dug out to make that runoff receptacle is now a hill to the side of Shaftesbury Lake.

A run-off from Coate Water follows Shaftesbury Avenue to a smaller lake near Nythe. From there it becomes Dorcan stream. Should Coate Water become too full, there are storm drains that can be opened allowing the water to flow all the way to Shaftesbury Lake. A footpath runs from Coate Water, parallel to the stream, that comes out at the lake.

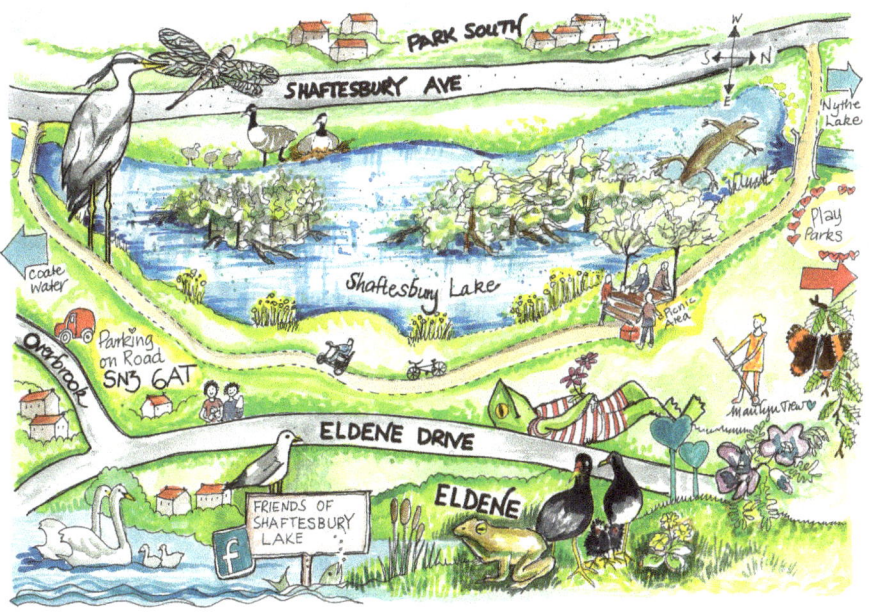

A happenchance Shaftesbury Lake may be. Yet, over the years, it's grown and matured into something rather lovely that's worth seeking out. A volunteer group have taken over care of the lake and the area around it, creating flowerbeds and planting bulbs. It's a credit to them. As with Liden lagoon there are geese, herons, ducks and a host of wildlife and biodiversity.

The work of the volunteer group began in 2018 with two people, Gail Collins and Pam Jones, with a common goal of improving the area for people and wildlife. Both Nythe, Eldene and Liden, and South Swindon parish councils support the group but they don't get any financial assistance. You can find out more about what they get up to on their Facebook group: https://www.facebook.com/groups/2626780270971128

SECTION THREE: CULTURE, CREAM TEAS AND A TRAIN

The Richard Jefferies Museum, Coate Water and the miniature railway

A place of joy, fun, delight and tranquillity, the Richard Jefferies museum is not, by their own admission, the easiest place to find. The Coate farmhouse, birthplace of Richard Jefferies, fronts a busy dual carriageway on the corner of Marlborough Road and Day House Lane with a postcode that takes you a mile up the road. It's opposite a Texaco garage and next door to the Sun Inn. But don't be deterred, for the museum is worth the effort.

The museum consists of a seventeenth century thatched cottage bought by the Jefferies family in 1800, a later, nineteenth century three-storied farmhouse, plus outbuildings, gardens, a copse, orchard and vegetable gardens. The site is run by the Richard Jefferies Museum Trust and is fully accredited by Arts Council England. Find out more on the museum's website: www.richardjefferies.org

What's in the museum?

The museum contains a sizeable collection of items related to Jefferies' life and work. There are first editions of much of Jefferies' writings along with photographs, paintings and memorabilia. Much of the house has undergone restoration to create the atmosphere of a mid-to-late 19th Century farmhouse.

The exhibits give fascinating insights into bygone times, sometimes bridging different layers of Swindon's rich history.

For example, a plaque placed on Liddington Hill in 1938 (with the support of the then Prime Minister, Neville Chamberlain) was later reputedly shot at by US troops in advance of their push into Nazi-occupied France during World War II.

If you think all that sounds a little dry, it's really not. The Richard Jefferies museum is a wonderful place for children and kids of all ages. The museum's garden is delightful. It's filled with elements from Jefferies' childrens' book Bevis, the chickens are often roaming free and it's a simply fabulous place for youngsters to stomp about. During term-time the museum runs

Nature Tots sessions for little ones. Visit their website or Facebook page for more details.

On summer Sundays the museum hosts cream teas and free music. And a whole host of other activities throughout the year: www.richardjefferies.org/what-s-on

The museum's garden backs onto the bottom end of Coate Water and they even have a Richard Jefferies railway halt for the Coate Water miniature railway. The RJ Halt tends to be operational on cream tea Sundays, sufficient volunteers allowing. With luck then you can stroll round Coate Water then take the train to the Richard Jefferies Museum. Enjoy a cream tea and then go back. Or vice versa.

The trains running on the Coate Water miniature railway are operated and maintained by the North Wilts Model Engineering Society. See coatewaterrailway.wixsite.com/swindon for full details. It's open on the first Saturday of the summer months, then every Sunday and bank holiday weekends (depending on the weather) from around 11am to 5pm – or dusk in the winter. During summer school holidays it's also open on Tuesdays.

The railway runs for just under a mile through a lovely wooded setting. A wheelchair accessible carriage is available if you ask. At the time of writing the fare is £2 per person for a ten-minute ride.

For the miniature railway geeks: this is a 5" and 7.25" dual gauge miniature railway with gradients of up to 1:57

NB: Steam haulage cannot be guaranteed as it's dependent on members bringing their locomotives.

Getting to the Richard Jefferies Museum and Opening Times
Richard Jefferies Museum
Marlborough Road, Coate Water, Swindon SN3 6AA
Telephone: 07768 917466

Email: info@richardjefferies.org

It's always best to check before you go. The museum is staffed by volunteers so opening times may vary, but the general opening times of the museum are as follows:

10:30 - 12:30 Tuesdays and Thursdays
10:00 - 16:00 Second Wednesday of each month
13:00 - 17:00 Every Sunday (from beginning of May to end of Sept)
www. richardjefferies.org/opening-times

On the Buses
Lots of buses - (e.g. 1, 1A, 3, 12, 13A, 14A) – run from Fleming Way in the town centre, a mere few minutes' walk from the railway station. Ask for the Sun Inn, Coate and the bus will drop you at the Texaco garage right across the road from the museum. The Coate Water underpass is about to be demolished and a road crossing installed.

After you have crossed the road, ahead of you you'll see the original gates to the country park. They stand there in splendid isolation as there's no fencing either side of them. A short distance up from the gates is a square bronze plaque on a stone. It commemorates Mrs Frances J Gay who, it tells us, served with distinction, for twenty-four years, the Richard Jefferies' Society.

Coate Water Country Park

Coate Water Park
Marlborough Rd
Swindon
SN3 6AA

Coate Water is a beautiful and much-loved country park situated 5km to the southeast of central Swindon, near junction 15 of the M4. The park began life as a reservoir formed to supply water to the nearby canal. In 1914 the canal was abandoned and the lake turned into a water park. There were changing rooms and a diving platform and later a 33-foot, Art Deco concrete diving platform.

The park boasts level and surfaced paths in and around the park and a route circumnavigating the entire lake – super for a steady stroll or a rigorous run. It's all pushchair and wheelchair friendly. Amongst the park's attractions are a children's playground, a summer splash park and an-all-year-round-café with a great reputation. I hear that the brownies are to die for and the chips rather good.

Coate Water is a nature reserve and a Site of Special Scientific Interest – so the park simply bursts with interesting bird and wildlife species and offers great fishing and bird-watching opportunities. It's reasonable to assume that Jefferies would have delighted in all that.

All that aside, Coate is where Richard Jefferies did much youthful stomping around. And it's a brilliant place for your youngsters to do the same. It's here where Jefferies' developed his passion for, and knowledge of, the natural environment. This country park is much more than a bit player in Bevis, The Story of a Boy – his book for children which is set entirely on and around the lake. A few yards past the play park you'll see an oak tree with a wooden sign by it, declaring it as the Council Oak described by Jefferies in Bevis.

Photo: Royston Cartwright

SECTION FOUR: MESSING ABOUT ON THE RIVER
OR RATHER
THE WILTS AND BERKS CANAL

WHENEVER I THINK of anything to do with boats and rivers and canals one of many antediluvian references, of which I might be over fond, comes to mind. In this instance it's a 1961 song, written by Tony Hatch and sung in the first instance by Josh McCrae. Ah! I remember it well:

> When the weather is fine then you know it's a sign
> For messing about on the river.
> If you take my advice there's nothing so nice
> As messing about on the river.
> There are long boats and short boats and all kinds of craft,
> And cruisers and keel boats and some with no draught.
> So take off your coat and hop in a boat
> Go messing about on the river.

Though, as indicated above, I'm in fact referring to a restored section of the Wilts and Berks Canal and Dragonfly – a delightful way to go messing about on the river.

There's an interesting aside in why the canal is called the

'Wilts and Berks' canal and not, as you might expect, The Wiltshire and Berkshire Canal. The story goes, that a lazy draughtsman, when drafting one of the Acts of Parliament for the canal, made the abbreviation for his own convenience. And it stuck! Thus by Parliamentary decree, the canal became the Wilts and Berks.

Under normal circumstances, Dragonfly excursions run from the landing stage at Waitrose in Wichelstowe. Its postcode is: SN1 7BX.

In the picture you see Dragonfly on the Waitrose side of the canal. Note the recently opened and really rather lovely footbridge linking to the Wichelstowe side and the Hall & Woodhouse pub/restaurant.

Organised and run by volunteers from the Wilts & Berks Canal Trust, a charming trip on the delightful Dragonfly runs from Wichelstowe to Kingshill and back – a round trip of around fifty minutes. There's a lift to allow wheelchair users and those with mobility issues to access the boat from the landing stage. Note though that there is only space for one wheelchair, and it's not

Photo: Chris Barry

possible to get larger powered wheelchairs on the lift.
It's a lovely trip – I've done it a couple of times. There's lots of wildlife to see on the canal – swans, herons, voles and more – and other points of interest that the skipper and crew will point out to you.
The season normally starts at Easter and finishes in September. Trips may extend through October depending on the weather. Then they start again in December for the ever-popular Santa trips.

Weekend public trips run at these times:
10.30am, 11.45am, 13.30pm and 14.45pm.

Fares:
£6 for adults
£3 for children

There must be a minimum ratio of one adult to three children.
You could turn up on a particular day/time and get lucky. But the boat is popular so if you're keen for a pleasure cruise then it's best to book. Bookings close at 7pm the day before you want to travel. If you don't have a confirmation email then you're not booked. To check details and to book visit their website: https://www.wbct.org.uk/enjoy-discover/take-a-boat-trip-with-us

NB: The above all applies in normal circumstances. But for the moment the trust can't run the usual boat trips because part of the canal is closed off to them. Instead they're offering Dragonfly Experiences. The fares for this are £3 per person regardless of age.

Trips run from 10.30am at weekends, at half-hourly intervals. To book, call the boat team on 07401 220076 or preferably email boat.bookings@wbct.org.uk.

A Bit About Dragonfly
Much like Ma Ramotswe of the No 1 Ladies Detective Agency, Dragonfly is traditionally built, with a steel hull and superstructure.

The engine has sound reduction so you get a smooth and quiet canal boat experience. She can carry up to twelve passengers and two crew members. She's roomy inside and has heating and a table so you can still enjoy a trip in poor weather. It's definitely best though in dry weather when you can enjoy the seating outside the cabin and get closer views of the wildlife.

The Footbridge

Installed in July 2019, the 35-metre length bridge crosses the Wilts and Berks Canal and links the Waitrose store on one side with the Hall and Woodhouse pub on the other. Designed by artist Sebastien Boyesen, in partnership with civil engineers Peter Brett Associates, the bridge is adorned with an eye-catching work of art. It features ornate laser cut steel panels, interspersed with coloured resin that reflect sunlight during daylight hours. Feature lights set in the handrail light the bridge up at night.

Photo: Chris Barry

SECTION FIVE: THE MAGIC ROUNDABOUT

MENTIONED IN THE introduction, that I set up my Born again Swindonian blog while studying for an English degree. The reason for the blog being, in no small part, to amass material for a travelling writing module I planned to study in my final year. What follows is an imagined entry for an imaginary Swindon guide-book featuring the Magic Roundabout as a tourist destination. Travel guides are often written from the viewpoint of the dispassionate observer – thus the style and tone of this piece is rather different from the rest of this book. Despite being a non-driver, I hold great affection for the Magic Roundabout because it, or at least my writing about it, helped me to a 1st class degree. Which is rather nice from a first-class traffic management system methinks.

THE MAGIC ROUNDABOUT

Dare you navigate yourself across the infamous & world-famous counter-flow 'Magic-Roundabout' – the 'white-knuckle' ride of traffic?

You'd be forgiven for being perplexed at the notion of a traffic roundabout being of any interest to anyone other than traffic-system aficionados. But you couldn't be more wrong. This fabled entity is known the world over.

Created in 1972, Swindon's Magic Roundabout was originally named the County Islands roundabout due to its location in close proximity to the town's County Ground football stadium, home of

Swindon Town FC. But the locals were not long in bestowing upon it the nickname 'The Magic Roundabout' after the TV programme of that name. Eventually the local authority submitted to the popular consensus and officially re-named the roundabout and gave it appropriate signage.

Swindon is famous, even infamous, for its roundabouts. But this legendary one surely has to be the jewel in the town's roundabout crown? Situated on a junction where five roads meet, the traffic-consuming monster vexes native visitors and utterly baffles those from across the pond. For all this though Swindonians love it and generally find their passage across it to be smooth and fluid, even at peak times.

The roundabout was created by the Road Research Laboratory (RRL) to deal with an area that was a motorist's nightmare, being routinely unable to handle the sheer volume of traffic converging on it from five directions. Like many of the best ideas their solution was stunning in its simplicity. They simply combined two roundabouts in one. The first being of the conventional clockwise type and the second, revolving inside the first, sending traffic anti-clockwise. This counter-flow roundabout solved the congestion problems back in the 1970s and is still, despite the ensuing increase in traffic volume over the last 40 years, processing it all as quickly and as smoothly as a giant Magimix.

Traffic keeps moving almost all the time, waiting only a few seconds to join each mini-roundabout and thus steadily travelling at low speed across the junction. A normal roundabout would involve long waits to join; signals would involve bursts of movement and long enforced stoppages. As a result, it has been calculated that the Magic Roundabout has a greater throughput of traffic than anything else that it would be possible to install in the same space. Magic indeed! Moreover, it has an excellent safety record.

Although voted the seventh worst junction in the UK, the roundabout's bark is worse than its bite. Though appearing difficult to negotiate, all it asks of the driver is to be observant and to always give priority to traffic coming from the right. One

GUIDE TO SWINDON

Photo: Richard Wintle

approach to the roundabout is to drive down Drove Road from Swindon's Old Town. If you don't fancy manoeuvring it in a car it's possible to stand and observe the carefully controlled mayhem from the safety of the pavement - you can even consume fish and chips from the chippy on the corner while you do.

Swindonians are very proud of their Magic Roundabout and the tourist information desk, situated in the town's central library on Regent Circus, sells a wide range of Magic Roundabout memorabilia that runs the range from key-rings to mugs to tea-towels and even T-shirts. So, if you've braved this colossal contraption of a road system you can celebrate your feat of derring-do with a suitable souvenir or two.

Whether you love it, hate it or are indifferent to it one thing is for sure: visit Swindon and you can't ignore it. Swindon-grown band XTC effectively and poetically capture the dizzying assault on the senses this behemoth can induce in their 1981 song: 'English Roundabout':

> ' ... all the horns go 'beep! beep!'
> All the people follow like sheep,
> I'm full of light and sound,
> Making my head go round, round.'

Or so it's alleged.

Appendix

Answers to New Swindon Kids' Quiz Trail

1. Cenotaph/war memorial. 1914 – 1918 &1939 – 1945
2. Squadron Leader Harold Starr and Wing Commander John Starr
3. W W
4. Isambard Kingdom Brunel. 29th March 1973
5. 42
6. Starts at Canal Walk/Cambria Bridge. Ends at West Leaze
7. The NHS. On the blue plaque on the front of the building.
8. 7
9. 3
10. 6 ft 6 inches or 2 metres. King class locomotives
11. 37
12. 1961
13. BRW RAA – BRITISH RAILWAYS WESTERN REGION ATHLETICS ASSOCIATION
14. Drawing office and lecture room
15. The railway cottage museum.
16. A phoenix or a griffin – it's unclear which. On the corner of the old Wilkinson's building.
17. Above the doorway of a public house that once stood alongside the canal when it was still in Swindon.

Answers to Old Town Kids' Quiz Trail

1. The sculpture is called Applause. The sculptor is called Mark Amis.
2. Stout
3. The Royal Oak
4. Sunflowers.

5. Westlecot Bowls Club
6. 25
7. A rabbit
8. The ladies' toilet
9. Thornbury House
10. Bath Methodist Church
11. Swindon Museum and Art Gallery/Apsley House
12. 1988
13. 94A/95A
14. a. 19
15. b. Blue
16. William Hall
17. 1st May 1818
18. A Lion

That's the end of the trail!

www.ingramcontent.com/pod-product-compliance
Lightning Source LLC
LaVergne TN
LVHW010308070426
835510LV00025B/3412